The Who's Who of the Anglo-Zulu War

The Who's Who of the Anglo-Zulu War

Part I

The British

by

Ian Knight and Adrian Greaves

Pen & Sword
MILITARY

First published in Great Britain in 2006 by
Pen & Sword Military
an imprint of
Pen & Sword Books Ltd
47 Church Street
Barnsley
South Yorkshire
S70 2AS

Typeset in 11/13 Sabon by
Lamorna Publishing Services

Printed and bound in England by
CPI UK

For a complete list of Pen & Sword titles please contact
PEN & SWORD BOOKS LIMITED
47 Church Street, Barnsley, South Yorkshire, S70 2AS, England
E-mail: enquiries@pen-and-sword.co.uk
Website: www.pen-and-sword.co.uk

Contents

Glossary

Afrikaans

Afrikaans – language spoken by the descendants of the original European settlers at the Cape; predominantly Dutch with the addition of some French, German, Indonesian and local African words and constructions.

Afrikaner – descendant of the first predominantly Dutch-speaking white settlers at the Cape. Often known as 'Boers'.

Boer – literally a country person or farmer, the common name applied to the descendants of the first white Dutch-speaking settlers at the Cape.

Drift – a ford or crossing place.

Laager – a defensive formation improvised by drawing wagons into a circle. Also used during the Anglo-Zulu War to refer to an entrenched or fortified position generally.

isiZulu

ibutho (pl. amabutho) – Zulu guild, grouped together according to the common-age of its members, providing part time national service to the Zulu kings or to other important amakhosi. Often translated in a military context as 'regiment'.

ikhanda (pl. amakhanda) – Zulu royal homestead (literal 'head', meaning of state authority) serving as an administrative centre and often as a barracks for amabutho.

impi – matters pertaining to war, or a group of men gathered together as an armed force.

induna (pl. izinduna) – a state functionary or official appointed to a position of authority by the Zulu king or other amakhosi.

inkosi (pl. amakhosi) – hereditary chief or ruler.

oNdini/Ulundi – alternative versions of the name of King Cetshwayo's principle royal homestead, from the common root *undi*, meaning 'a high place'. The residence was commonly known as oNdini by the Zulus; Lord Chelmsford initially used this version in correspondence but once the campaign was underway took to calling it Ulundi. The battle which took place there on 4 July is generally referred to by this name.

umuzi (pl. imizi) – ordinary Zulu family homestead.

Foreword

Like many other Victorian wars, less well-remembered today, the Anglo-Zulu War of 1879 was a bitterly contested and savage war, where prisoners were seldom taken, and which was fought out over rugged terrain and in the extremes of African weather. While the politics of the war reflect an age very different from our own, the human cost remains readily comprehensible. The bald statistics give some impression of the scale of the conflict, small by the standards of suffering of the great European and American wars of the century, yet significant enough to give a shudder even to the greatest military power of the age. According to the official history, a total of over 12,000 British and Colonial troops participated in this hard-fought campaign, of whom seventy-six officers and 1,007 British and Colonial troops were killed in action, and thirty-seven officers and 206 men wounded. At least 604 African auxiliaries were killed fighting for the British – a figure that is probably significantly underestimated. A further seventeen officers and 330 men died of disease during the war, and throughout 1879 a total of ninety-nine officers and 1,286 men were invalided 'from the command for causes incidental to the campaign'.

During the six months of the Zulu War a total of 53,851 medical treatments were recorded, most for disease, many for minor injuries, sunburn or stomach disorders, and some for injuries sustained during combat. There were makeshift army hospitals at Durban, Pietermaritzburg, Ladysmith and Utrecht;

the doctors were mostly drawn from the Army Medical Department, the support staff from the Army Hospital Corps – and a number of civilian nurses who volunteered for the job in England.

While for the British the war was merely one element in their struggle to maintain a global Empire – the professional soldiers themselves moved on to other wars, the politicians to other intrigues and crises – the impact on the Zulu people was permanent and devastating. It is estimated that over 40,000 Zulu men fought in defence of their country, and as many as 10,000 were killed. In addition the king was deposed, the state infrastructure destroyed, hundreds of ordinary homes burned by the invaders and thousands of head of cattle looted.

The lives of individuals caught up in the war reflected these different realities. The bright burst of headlines that heralded the war produced the inevitable crop of heroes and villains who became household names in Britain, but for most participation in the war was an anonymous affair. The service of the majority of ordinary British soldiers was often recorded in only the briefest of official records, while that of the Zulus was scarcely recognized beyond the confines of their immediate families. Yet the impact of all wars is, above all, a human one, and the purpose of these two volumes is to assess something of that impact upon the lives of a small number of those individuals who took part – and, indeed, to assess their impact upon it. It is primarily intended as a companion piece for students and readers of the conflict, and it makes no claims to comprehensiveness. Even to provide biographical details of all British officers who took part – whose lives are arguably the best documented – would require a much larger work than this. Instead, we offer a selection of experiences which we hope is, in some way, representative, and our criteria for inclusion has, on occasion, been arbitrary. While we have tried to include all of the major figures, the movers and shakers who shaped the conflict, we have also included many individuals whose lives appeared to us particularly interesting or, in the case of the Colonials and Zulus in volume II, could be adequately documented.

We are grateful for the help we have received in researching this work, both from students of the war, and from the descendants of those involved. Lee Stevenson has most generously made available his own meticulous research into the lives of veterans of the battle of Rorke's Drift, while Ian Woodason – who runs a website dedicated to the graves and memorials of those who fought in the war – also made free with his own inspiring archives. So too did Ian Castle. Ian Knight would like to acknowledge his particular debt to his old friend and mentor, the late 'SB' Bourquin, who first opened a road for him into the green hills of Zululand.

This work is dedicated to all who participated in this campaign, be they British, Colonial or Zulu, great men or small, brave and not so brave; all fought in the honest belief that what they were doing was right.

Ian Knight and Adrian Greaves.
Chichester and Tenterden, 2006

Introduction

The Anglo-Zulu War of 1879

On 11 December 1878, before the unblinking lens of a local photographer, a party of colonial officials met a group of envoys from the Zulu kingdom beneath the spreading branches of a clump of wild fig trees on the Natal bank of the Thukela River. It was indeed an historic occasion, worthy of recording for posterity, for it was the moment when the threads that entwined the twin histories of the Zulu kingdom and the British Empire in southern Africa finally entangled both irrevocably in conflict. For the Zulus, the purpose of the meeting was to hear an independent report into a disputed boundary; the colonial officials, however, had a more sinister agenda. Attached to the boundary commission's findings were a series of demands that amounted to an ultimatum, specifically designed to destroy the political independence of the Zulu people.

The Zulu kingdom had emerged in the first quarter of the nineteenth century. The African communities lived along the fertile and well-watered eastern seaboard of southern Africa, between the Kahlamba Mountains – known to the first white explorers as the Drakensberg or 'Dragon Mountains' – and the Indian Ocean. Out of dozens of groups speaking broadly the same language and following broadly the same pastoral lifestyle, the Zulu, who lived on the middle reaches of the White Mfolozi River, had become dominant. Under their controversial king, Shaka kaSenzangakhona, they extended their influence from the Phongolo River in the north to the Thukela in the south, and disrupted the lives and political affiliations of those further beyond. While the old chiefdoms retained their identities, they were brought under the political control of the Zulu Royal House, and their young men required to serve in the part-time citizen militias – the *amabutho* system – controlled by the Zulu king. A new, infinitely more complex, militarily robust and economically powerful African state had emerged, even on the very eve of European penetration.

Whites had first come to southern Africa in the seventeenth century, when the Dutch had established a small way-station at the tip of the Continent, the Cape of Good Hope, to service their ships on the long sea haul to their profitable imperial possessions in the East Indies. The Dutch had easily displaced the original inhabitants at the Cape, the semi-nomadic Khoi and San people, but had little interest in expanding into the interior. Over the centuries however, their settlement, swollen by French and German political refugees from Europe, achieved a momentum of its own, expanding slowly according to the needs of its frontier farmers for new grazing lands. By the end of the eighteenth century it had collided with a stronger African group, the amaXhosa, along the banks of the Great Fish River, and the scene was set for nearly a century of frontier conflicts that would have much in common with the history of the American West.

The British assumed control of the Cape in 1806, in one of the twists and turns which marked the progress of their global war against Napoleon Bonaparte. The British, too, had a largely maritime mindset, and were primarily interested in safeguarding their own strategic oceanic highways, but their arrival precipitated changes within the settler dynamic of the Cape. Many of the original Dutch settlers, particularly on the exposed Eastern Frontier, remained unreconciled to British rule, and began to explore the possibility of a move into the interior. Simultaneously, the Cape became a focus for the upsurge of commercial exploration which marked the end of the Napoleonic wars as unemployed British soldiers and sailors, representatives now of the undisputed world power, sought to discover and exploit new markets.

Ironically it was the very success of King Shaka's kingdom which first attracted the Europeans, the harbingers of its destruction. Garbled rumours of the rise of the Zulu people, of their wealth and power, spread to the Cape and attracted the attention of the Cape merchants. In 1824 a small group of predominantly British adventurers braved the sandbar across the mouth of the so-called 'Bay of Natal' and established a tiny trading enclave. They prospered under King Shaka's patronage, trading exotic imported goods – beads and blankets – for the Zulus' cattle and hides. Allowed to thrive as a client chiefdom, they took African wives and accumulated African followers, hunted, traded, squabbled among themselves and with their neighbours, and between them conspired to blacken King Shaka's name to posterity. Their ramshackle settlement grew in time into the modern city of Durban; to such anarchic beginnings did all British interests in the eastern seaboard belong.

Initially, the Government in London showed little interest in extending its official protection over the settlement, but by the 1830s the reluctance of the Dutch settlers at the Cape to remain under British control had led to a flood of immigration into the interior which the authorities struggled to contain. The passage of the Boer diaspora was marked with conflicts with African groups – including the Zulus – and raised the spectre of an outside foreign influence in the Cape's back yard. To forestall such an eventuality, British troops were dispatched to secure Port Natal and, after a curious little skirmish with the Boers among the mangrove swamps and sand dunes on the shores of the bay in 1842, the British annexed the area immediately south of the Zulu kingdom. It was known officially as the colony of Natal, after the name first given to the area by the Portuguese explorer Vasco da Gama on Christmas Day 1497, *Terra Natalis*, the land seen on the day of Christ's birth.

For decades the British administration was haphazard and the number of white settlers small and vastly outnumbered by the African population among whom they lived. Many of those African groups were linked by a history of animosity with the Zulu Royal House north across the Thukela River; they were either resistors of Shaka's attempts to incorporate them into the Zulu kingdom, dislocated survivors of his military incursions or, increasingly, political refugees from Zululand itself. None of these groups had ever been conquered by the British – they had, in effect, reached an accommodation with British interests in which the underlying common interest was a rejection of Zulu royal authority. Nonetheless, for thirty years British Natal and independent Zululand enjoyed a broadly harmonious relationship, and indeed the most vibrant elements in the sluggish colonial economy were largely dependant upon the extraction of resources from Zululand itself.

In the 1870s, the political geography began to change again, stimulated by the discovery of diamonds in the nominally independent – but not for long – territory of Griqualand West in 1868. The realization that southern Africa might possess hitherto unsuspected mineral reserves stimulated the British to find a broader geo-political solution to an area which had remained stubbornly parochial and resolutely argumentative. The Cape's strategic role had not yet faded – the potential threat was no longer French men-of-war but Russian gunboats, an unlikely manifestation of the 'Great Game' for control of India – but Africa suddenly offered a return on Britain's investment. Yet if the diamond economy was to be exploited fully, goods and expertise would need to move freely into Africa through the Cape and Port Natal (by now renamed Durban) and on into the limitless interior, while African labour moved towards the mines in return. Imperial visionaries dreamed of a level of infrastructure that was simply not possible given the fragmented political loyalties of the 1870s.

4

Southern Africa remained a hotbed of mutually antagonistic British colonies, Afrikaner republics and beleaguered indigenous kingdoms.

The solution, conceived in London, was called Confederation – a bringing of these disparate groups under a loose British authority with a view to expanding their political and economic common ground. In 1877 a new British High Commissioner, a statesman highly experienced in Anglo-Indian affairs, Sir Henry Bartle Frere, was sent to the Cape specifically to implement the Confederation policy. London recognized, of course, that Confederation implied an inherent risk of military force, but Frere was required to use it sparingly, and if possible to avoid the evils of a war against the Boer settler states. Not that the London Government was primarily motivated by humanitarian reservations about the justice of any war in southern Africa; with tension looming with Russia over the tortured question of influence in Afghanistan, it was worried about stretching its resources too thinly upon the ground.

Frere found the situation at the Cape worryingly volatile. The British had already annexed the bankrupt Transvaal Republic, but it was essential that anti-British sentiments among the Boers was not allowed to fester. In addition, a wave of unrest among the area's black communities, a common reaction to half a century of political and economic marginalization, threatened to destabilize the region's frontier zones. Frere soon became convinced that a demonstration of British determination was necessary to shore up their faltering authority and to force the pace of Confederation. Advised by officials on the spot, Frere soon came to believe that the Zulu kingdom offered the most constructive target for cost-effective military action. Zululand was the most powerful and economically robust African kingdom left standing south of the Limpopo River. It maintained an army – of sorts – its king refused his young men permission to work at the diamond mines, and the European missionary community portrayed the administration as hostile, barbarian and attached to a way of life Frere considered deeply anachronistic. Towards the end of 1878 Frere seized upon a festering boundary dispute, which had dragged on for decades between the Transvaal and Zululand, and a series of minor border infringements, to provoke a war with the Zulu king. His actions were not entirely supported by London, but Frere expected a successful conclusion to the war before London had time to object.

It was a tragic miscalculation. The Zulu king, Cetshwayo kaMpande, was a nephew of the founding father, King Shaka. He had worked, since his accession in 1873, to maintain a cordial relationship with Natal, but while he was mystified by the sudden change in British attitudes, he was a traditionalist who was not ready to abandon the ways of his people. The Zulu army was not professional in the manner of its British counterpart, but the king could call upon the service of the nation's manpower, assembled into part-time militias known as *amabutho*. They were principally armed with shields and spears, as they had been in King Shaka's day, but they also possessed thousands of antiquated firearms – dumped on the world market by European powers as they became obsolete – and the men were motivated, as 1878 passed, by a growing sense of indignation at British presumption. According to British intelligence reports, compiled on the eve of the invasion, the Zulu army was over 40,000 men strong; although, in the event, the king was never able to assemble much more than half that number at any given place and time, as an estimate of the total number of men who would at some point during the war take up arms, it was not so very far wide of the mark.

Frere presented his ultimatum on the banks of the Thukela – the Natal/Zulu border – on 11 December 1878. It was drafted to allow little room for King Cetshwayo to manoeuvre; and Frere expected it to be rejected. The task of breaking up the Zulu kingdom was to fall to Britain's senior military commander in southern Africa, Lieutenant General Lord Chelmsford. Middle-aged, conservative, a product of the British military establishment, Chelmsford was nonetheless a conscientious officer experienced in colonial warfare. He understood the urgency in Frere's political imperative – to defeat the Zulus and intimidate opposition to Confederation elsewhere in the region before London could object to the means – and planned the campaign accordingly. Like most Victorian commanders, he had to face the task with too few resources for the job, a handful of regular infantry battalions, a couple of artillery batteries and too few cavalrymen, all of the latter colonial troops. Even the eventual and reluctant agreement of the Natal authorities to authorize the raising of an African auxiliary force from among its black population – the Natal Native Contingent – scarcely allayed his shortage of manpower. Chelmsford initially planned to invade Zululand from five separate points along the Natal and Transvaal borders, each column converging on the cluster of royal home-steads at oNdini, in the heart of Zululand, which constituted King Cetshwayo's capital. In the events, Chelmsford could not assemble the logistical support necessary to sustain this ambitious plan; not only was he short of men, but white South Africa could not offer him sufficient baggage wagons with which to feed his columns on the move. He was forced to reduce his offensive columns to three, and to keep the other two in supportive roles.

The starting points for his invasion were a series of well-worn highways, which had for a generation served as the entry points into the Zulu kingdom from the colonies. One column (the Right Flank or No. 1 Column, commanded by Colonel Pearson) assembled at the Lower Drift on the Thukela River, in Zululand's lush coastal belt. A supportive column (No. 2, commanded by Brevet Colonel Durnford) was placed upstream of Pearson, above the Middle Drift on the Thukela. The Centre Column (No. 3, commanded by Colonel Glyn, but accompanied by Chelmsford himself) assembled at Rorke's Drift on the Mzinyathi (Buffalo) River. The Left Flank Column (No. 4, commanded by Colonel Wood) entered via the disputed territory lying between the Transvaal and Zululand in the north, while the final supportive column (Colonel

Rowlands' No. 5 Column) was placed on the northern Transvaal/Zulu/Swazi border. The offensive columns (1, 3 and 4) numbered roughly 3,000 men each, of whom only half were British regulars wearing the famous 'red coat'.

Chelmsford's strategy was framed by the need for a swift and decisive campaign, and indeed he was nagged by doubts that the Zulus would avoid a direct confrontation, and would instead drag out the war by attempting a guerrilla response. Frere's ultimatum expired on 11 January, and despite the difficulty of coordinating their movements, Chelmsford's lumbering columns managed to push across onto Zulu soil on three fronts. On the 12th, Chelmsford himself led a foray from the Centre Column, which destroyed the homestead belonging to an important border *inkosi* (chief), a favourite of the king's named Sihayo kaXongo. Chelmsford thought the campaign began well enough; at that point he knew nothing of King Cetshwayo's plans or movements.

Chelmsford was destined soon to be disabused. While the king had ordered many Zulu men living in the border districts to remain to watch the British movements, he had assembled the main body of the *amabutho* – perhaps 30,000 men – at oNdini. Determined to portray himself as the victim of British aggression, which he was, the king had allowed the invaders to seize the initiative. Once it became clear that the Centre Column was particularly active in attacking the king's supporters in the vulnerable border districts, Cetshwayo and his military council decided to direct their main response against it. On the afternoon of 17 January, after several days of ritual preparation, the Zulu army left the vicinity of oNdini. A small section broke away to reinforce those men remaining in the coastal sector; the rest, perhaps as many as 25,000, marched west towards Lord Chelmsford's column advancing from Rorke's Drift.

The Zulu reaction fell upon the British on all fronts beginning from 22 January – a day, ironically, which the Zulu believed was one of ill omen. On the coast, Pearson's column was just crossing the Nyezane River early on the morning of

22nd when it blundered into about 6,000 men commanded by one of the king's appointed generals, Godide kaNdlela. For an hour or so it looked as if Pearson's men might just be out-flanked but in the end the Zulu superiority in numbers was just too low and the British firepower too great. The Zulus withdrew, and that same day Pearson continued his advance towards Eshowe. In the north of the country, Colonel Wood also found himself drawn into a running fight with local Zulu royalists, the abaQulusi, which spluttered on for several days around the Qulusi strongholds of the Zungwini and Hlobane mountains.

It was on the Centre Column, however, that the blow fell heaviest. On 20th, Chelmsford had moved forward from Rorke's Drift, and had established a new camp at the foot of a distinctive rocky outcrop known as Isandlwana. That same day, rumours reached him of the Zulu advance from oNdini, and he resolved to probe a line of hills ahead of him. Late on the evening of 21st, one of his patrols encountered a Zulu force in the hills above the Mangeni River gorge, about twelve miles in front of Isandlwana. Thinking this was the main Zulu army, Chelmsford decided to split his force, moving out immediately from Isandlwana with a mobile column, hoping to intercept the Zulus at dawn on 22nd. He left a sizable detachment at Isandlwana to guard the column's baggage train and tents; almost as an afterthought, he ordered elements of Colonel Durnford's No. 2 Column up to Isandlwana in support.

In fact, Chelmsford's reconnaissance had merely intercepted local Zulu troops moving towards a rendezvous with the main army. The main body, commanded by one of the king's most trusted generals, Ntshingwayo kaMahole, had in fact already passed across Chelmsford's front and, even as he moved out from Isandlwana on the morning of 22nd, was lying close to the camp to the north-east, screened only by the undulating country in between. It was discovered at about 11.30 a.m. by elements of Durnford's command, which had only recently arrived at Isandlwana.

The encounter caught both sides off-guard. The Zulu

amabutho, fuelled by their collective anger at the British invasion, rushed forward to attack while the British commanders attempted to deploy in a defensive position. It was the Zulus who seized the initiative, perhaps because their regimental commanders had been well into a command briefing when the initial clash took place. The Zulu attack took place rapidly over a wide area, making good use of the traditional Zulu encircling tactics. The British, however, were unprepared for such an extensive attack, and their own positions were poorly chosen and widely scattered. Initially the British held their ground but their outlying detachments were forced to withdraw for fear of being cut off. At about 1 p.m., as the British attempted to withdraw upon their tents, their line collapsed. Their infantry companies were driven back then pinned in place by the encircling Zulu 'horns'; at the foot of Isandlwana, and in the broken stream-beds beyond, the redcoats at Isandlwana were overwhelmed. Durnford and his colleague, Lieutenant Colonel Pulleine, were killed, together with over 1,300 of the camp's 1,700 defenders. The overwhelming majority of the British survivors were African auxiliaries.

In the aftermath of Isandlwana, a number of Zulu *amabutho* held in reserve during the battle pressed forward to the Mzinyathi River – the border with Natal – to cut the British line of retreat. In accordance with his defensive strategy, the king had ordered his men not to cross into Natal, but the opportunity to loot the abandoned farms and African homesteads across the river proved too powerful to a large group commanded by Prince Dabulamanzi kaMpande. Crossing the river downstream from Rorke's Drift, about 3,500 of them moved towards a supply depot established at a Swedish mission by Lord Chelmsford. The garrison – scarcely 150 men, commanded by Lieutenants Chard and Bromhead – decided to fortify the mission post with the stockpile of stores, rather than face the uncertainties of retreat in the open. They had scarcely surrounded the buildings with barricades made from sacks of corn and boxes of army biscuit when the Zulu vanguard arrived. A running fight developed which lasted throughout the evening and into the night. The Zulus drove the defenders out of one building – an improvised hospital – but their attacks faltered in the early hours in the face of desperate resistance around the last remaining building. Sometime before dawn the Zulus withdrew, leaving as many as 600 dead scattered around the post and on their line of retreat. Just seventeen of the British garrison were killed in nearly ten hours of fighting.

The defence of Rorke's Drift was undeniably gallant, and it presented Lord Chelmsford with something of a propaganda coup. The general himself had finally become aware that something had occurred at Isandlwana, and had marched back from the Mangeni hills to find the camp overrun and the defenders slaughtered. With his own men exhausted and with no clear intelligence on the Zulu movements, he had little option but to spend a dreadful night, lying among the freshly dead on the stricken field; the following morning he had returned to Rorke's Drift, where his invasion had begun less than a fortnight before. The discovery that the Rorke's Drift post had held, at least vanquished the immediate fear of a Zulu invasion of Natal, and allowed him to temper his dispatches home with a rousing report of British heroism.

Yet the bald fact was that the war had begun disastrously. The Centre Column had been driven out of Zululand, and lacked the capacity, at least in the short term, to regain the initiative. The flanking columns, left unsupported, could not hope to carry on the invasion by themselves while widespread panic gripped the settler community in Natal, and outlying farmers flocked to the dubious safety of the towns. Chelmsford could not expect outside reinforcements for weeks – if at all – and for several days the British war-effort seemed in danger of falling apart altogether. And it might have done so, had King Cetshwayo been able to administer a further sharp blow in quick succession.

It was to prove the Zulus' tragedy that he could not. On all fronts the Zulu forces had been largely exhausted by the fighting of 22-24 January, and their concentrations had soon dispersed. Over a thousand men had been killed at Isandlwana alone, and perhaps as many again mortally wounded. A number of chiefs and sons of chiefs had been killed, and the total Zulu losses, including the fighting at Rorke's Drift, at Nyezane and around Hlobane, may have run to 4,000 men. The nation was shocked and in mourning; the king could not hope to re-assemble the *amabutho* for many weeks.

And while King Cetshwayo pondered his options, Lord Chelmsford slowly regained the initiative. News of the defeat brought shock to London and while, in due course, it would call the actions of both Frere and Chelmsford into searching question, Imperial honour needed to be regained. Reinforcements were hurried to Natal. In the coastal sector, Colonel Pearson's column, which had occupied a deserted Norwegian mission station at Eshowe the day following Nyezane, decided to hold their ground. To King Cetshwayo's indignation, they dug in, turning Eshowe into the most impressive earthwork constructed by the British during the Zululand campaign. Isolated thirty miles inside Zulu territory, they were cut off by Zulu patrols, and for more than two months they lived on reduced rations in cramped and insanitary conditions, completely out of touch with the events of the wider war. And yet by doing so they maintained a British presence on Zulu soil, tied up large numbers of Zulu troops from the coastal districts, and gave something of the illusion that the war was being waged aggressively.

By the middle of March, the war was poised to enter a new active phase. It was heralded in the north where, like Pearson, Colonel Wood had endeavoured to make his presence felt. Wood had engaged in a low-intensity war of raid and counter raid with local Zulu elements, particularly the abaQulusi and the followers of an exiled Swazi prince, Mbilini waMswati, who had emerged as one of the most daring guerrilla leaders on the Zulu side. The catalyst was an incident that took place outside the exposed frontier settlement of Lüneburg on 12 March. A garrison had been established at Lüneburg to protect the white community, and it was supplied by a tortuous line of communication extending into the Transvaal. In early March a convoy of eighteen supply and ammunition wagons had run into difficulties in the Ntombe River valley outside Lüneburg. A detachment of the 80th Regiment under a Captain Moriarty had been sent from Lüneburg to escort the wagons in, but bad weather had left them stranded at the river itself. The camp was poorly placed and the men demoralized, and at dawn on 12 March the convoy was the subject of a surprise attack by some 800 men led by Prince Mbilini himself. The camp was overrun and Moriarty and some seventy of his men were killed.

In response, Colonel Wood was determined to make a strike against the abaQulusi, whom he regarded as Mbilini's main supporters. The timing of his response was conditioned by a request from Lord Chelmsford, who had assembled troops on the coast to march to the relief of Eshowe, and who asked for a diversion to draw off Zulu attention. Wood decided to attack the Hlobane mountain complex with the mounted elements from his column at dawn on 28 March. His idea was to assault the mountain from either end, driving across the summit, dispersing the abaQulusi sheltering there, and carrying off their not inconsiderable herd of cattle. Although his assault parties were in position before dawn, the attack went badly wrong from the start. One party failed to ascend the mountain at all, while Wood and his staff, following behind as observers, came under fire; two of Wood's personal staff were killed. The other party successfully reached the summit of Hlobane, but found its line of retreat cut by the abaQulusi behind it. At the height of the battle, a large Zulu army came expectedly into view. This was the main Zulu strike force – the same *amabutho* that had triumphed at Isandlwana – and which the king had only recently reassembled. Since Pearson's column was already isolated, the Zulu high command had decided to direct this fresh effort against Wood's column. The army was already approaching Wood's base at Khambula when Wood rode out to attack Hlobane. The army's arrival during the action was coincidental, but it immediately made Wood's assault untenable. Wood himself returned to Khambula, leaving his assault parties to make their way off Hlobane as best they could. The men on the summit had few enough options; the main body was forced into a hair-raising descent of a rocky staircase later known as the Devil's Pass, while others scattered and promptly ran into *amabutho* coming in the opposite direction. The assault on Hlobane collapsed into a rout and cost the lives of over seventy officers and men.

It did at least, however, provide obvious warning of the Zulu intentions. The following morning Wood ensured that the camp at Khambula – a chain of fortified wagon-laagers and entrenchments running along a narrow ridge – was in complete readiness for defence. The Zulu army moved out from its overnight bivouac near Hlobane and by late morning had begun to deploy for the attack. As it moved to surround the camp on all sides, Wood noticed that the Zulu right horn appeared to be more advanced than the rest of the army. Seizing the opportunity to provoke an uncoordinated attack, he sent his mounted troops (survivors of Hlobane) out to sting it into launching an unsupported assault. It was a devastatingly effective move, for the discipline of the right 'horn' dissolved under fire, and the men rushed forward, only to be met by a hail of British fire. Although some elements reached the wagons – only to be shot down – the rest retired just as the rest of the Zulu army hurried forward. For several hours Wood faced a series of determined attacks on all sides, but their initial failure robbed the Zulus of the chance to maintain the initiative. Wood was able to move his firepower to face each attack in turn. When, at last, the Zulu attacks faltered, Wood dispatched his mounted men who drove the *amabutho* away in a particularly brutal pursuit.

The Battle of Khambula was to prove a turning point in the war. The *amabutho*, who had advanced with the triumphant shout that 'we are the boys from Isandlwana!' suffered as many as 2,000 dead and hundreds more wounded. For the first time in the war, they had engaged in a major battle and been unquestionably defeated. And there was worse to come; even

14

as the battle was taking place, Lord Chelmsford had crossed the Thukela at the head of a relief column heading for Eshowe. On 2 April, he had deployed his command in a square on a wet grassy rise known as kwaGingindlovu and dispersed an attack by the Zulu forces investing Eshowe. The following day Eshowe was relieved, and within days Chelmsford had withdrawn his command to safer positions closer to the Natal border.

The twin defeats at either end of the country had not only caused the Zulus devastating losses (which, unlike the British, they could not replace) but also allowed the British the ascendancy on both fronts. The king and many of his councillors came increasingly to suspect that the war simply could not be won in the field, but when King Cetshwayo tentatively began to attempt to open negotiations with the British, another unpleasant truth became gradually clear to him. With the war at last going his way, Lord Chelmsford had little incentive to adopt a negotiated settlement before he had gained his revenge for Isandlwana.

The victories at Khambula and Gingindlovu allowed Chelmsford to complete the plans for a new invasion of Zululand, which his reinforcements now allowed him to undertake. Throughout April and May he greatly strengthened his troops in the coastal sector, and assembled a new column, made up of troops freshly arrived from England, on the Ncome River, north of Rorke's Drift. The enlarged coastal column was re-designated the 1st Division, and the new column the 2nd. Wood's old column was re-designated the Flying Column, and directed to advance in tandem with the 2nd Division. With his preparations almost complete, Chelmsford – who still needed all the transport he could get – was forced to face the spectre of Isandlwana. On 21 May he authorized the first major burial expedition to the old battlefield, where the corpses of the slain – variously picked clean by ants, or mummified by the sun – were hastily covered over, and those serviceable wagons which remained in the camp area were brought away.

The new invasion began on 1 June 1879 and went badly

from the start. The exiled Prince Imperial of France, Louis Napoleon, who was accompanying the force as an unofficial observer, was ambushed while patrolling ahead of the 2nd Division's advance, and was killed. The incident itself was a minor one, the fortunes of war, but the Prince's status ensured that it caused a scandal in the British and European press at the very time Lord Chelmsford was struggling to put the Isandlwana debacle behind him.

In the event, the second invasion was slow and thorough. On the coast, the defeat at Gingindlovu had largely destroyed the Zulu will to resist, and as the 1st Division ponderously advanced, it destroyed royal homesteads without opposition and negotiated with regional *amakhosi* for their surrender. There was more opposition in the heart of the country, and the 2nd Division and Flying Column advanced in the face of constant skirmishing. By the end of June, however, they had reached the heights overlooking the White Mfolozi River, and had destroyed the venerable royal homesteads in the emaKhosini valley, where Shaka's ancestors were buried. By the beginning of July Chelmsford had reached the Mfolozi River. There was a last minute flurry of diplomatic activity as King Cetshwayo attempted to ward off the catastrophe, but there was never any hope that a final confrontation could be avoided. Lord Chelmsford, indeed, was spurred on by the knowledge that London had sent out someone to replace him, and he was determined to have his victory before he lost his command.

On 3 July Chelmsford's mounted troops crossed the river to scout out a position for the coming battle. They very nearly fell into a skilful Zulu ambush, but returned with the intelligence Chelmsford required. The following morning Chelmsford marched over 5,000 men – regulars and auxiliaries, including lancers, artillery and Gatling guns – out of his forward camp, crossed the river, and formed up in a hollow-square four ranks deep. The square marched to a selected position on the undulating plain between a circle of royal homesteads, close to oNdini itself. Their plans had been obvious enough to the Zulu army, who had been gathering over the preceding week. Now, the *amabutho* emerged from their overnight bivouacs and as the morning sun burned off the last of the mist, they moved to attack. At 400 yards they were met by a withering blast of rifle and machine-gun fire that checked many of them; some elements of the left 'horn' mounted a determined attack which pressed to within a few yards of a corner of the square before being scythed down, but for the most part they were unable to brave that terrible fire zone. After less than an hour Chelmsford recognized that they were faltering, and dispatched his cavalry to drive them from the field. By the time the last warriors were driven from the surrounding hilltops, the British had already set fire to the great royal homesteads, oNdini among them.

Chelmsford saw no need to remain on the field; by lunchtime he had withdrawn his men across the river, and within days he had resigned his command. Even as the children, wives and mothers of the Zulu dead had emerged from their hiding places to search for the remains of their loved ones in the great circle of corpses in the long grass on the Ulundi plain, Chelmsford was on his way home.

His successor, General Sir Garnet Wolseley, was irritated by Chelmsford's haste to be gone. He regarded his withdrawal as premature; the whereabouts of King Cetshwayo was unknown, and no attempt had been made to pacific the country as a whole. Reorganizing Chelmsford's forces, Wolseley dispatched large patrols to search for the king, and sent columns to the central border and the Ntombe valley, to intimidate the most recalcitrant *amakhosi*. On 28 August a party of Dragoons finally captured King Cetshwayo in the Ngome forest; the last shots of the war were fired near Lüneburg a week later.

Wolseley had already disposed of King Cetshwayo's kingdom and had determined to send the king into exile. In accordance with his political brief to prevent the united Zulu kingdom posing further threat to British interests, Wolseley had decided to break it up into what he believed to be its constituent parts.

17

A change of administration in London, from Conservative to Liberal, meant there was no public will for annexation; the Confederation policy, upon the success of which Frere had gambled so much, had been abandoned. Frere himself was recalled, and Zululand was left to its own devices. It was divided up among thirteen *amakhosi* appointed by Wolseley – a classic example of divide and rule.

The British invasion of 1879 had been a brutal and bloody affair, costly far beyond the expectation of the men who engineered it. Yet, for all the thousands of dead, the destroyed homesteads and looted cattle, the true cost to the Zulus would only become apparent in the years afterwards. The invasion was but the first step in a sustained attack on the old Zulu order, on the representatives of the House of Shaka, and ultimately upon the Zulu way of life. For many Zulus who had fought so hard to resist the British, the representatives of the new order were little more than traitors, and the country gradually divided between those who accepted the reality of defeat, and those who advocated a return of the king. Violence between the British appointees, and between the appointees and the royalists living among them, became commonplace. By 1881 it was clear that on one level at least – that of maintaining order – Wolseley's settlement was a failure. In England, the image of King Cetshwayo, lodged in captivity at the Cape, had undergone a reinvention, and the anger unleashed by Isandlwana had begun to give way to a sense of unease about the justice or otherwise of the invasion. In 1882 King Cetshwayo was allowed to visit London, and granted an audience with Queen Victoria at Osborne House on the Isle of Wight. On finding that the terrible savage depicted in the illustrated press in 1879 was in fact a rather regal figure, now dressed smartly in European clothes, the British public cheered the Zulu king in the streets.

In a bizarre reversal of former policy, the Liberal administration decided to partition Zululand and restore King Cetshwayo to part of his own territory. However, he was not allowed to revive the *amabutho* system, and large tracts of his country were set aside for those who had waxed fat in his absence. He returned to Zululand in February 1883, but his restoration proved a disaster. While the king attempted to rebuild his old oNdini residence, friction between his supporters and his enemies escalated. In July 1883 he was suddenly attacked by his erstwhile general, *inkosi* Zibhebhu kaMaphitha, and oNdini once again was put to the torch. It is a testament to the bitter divisions engendered by the British invasion that in the fighting over fifty of the great Zulu nobles of the old kingdom were slaughtered, and by their own countrymen who they had fought alongside, on the same ground, just four years before.

King Cetshwayo fled to the sanctuary offered by British officials in Eshowe, but within months he was dead, apparently from heart failure. His death marked the true end of the chain of events ushered in by the conquest, but the repercussions tormented Zululand for several years yet. The mantle of royalist aspirations fell to his son, Dinuzulu, who invited Boer participation in an attempt to defeat Zibhebhu. They agreed and Zibhebhu was duly defeated at the Battle of Tshaneni in June 1884, but the cost of the victory was high. The Boers demanded so much land in payment that even the British were forced to intervene to curb their demands, and in 1887 the majority of Zululand was finally annexed to the British Crown. The young King Dinuzulu continued to resist and in 1888 led a rebellion in the forlorn hope of sweeping back the tide of European encroachment; it was a scrappy affair compared with the events of 1879, and ultimately as doomed. The leaders of the uprising, Dinuzulu and his uncles, were arrested and sent to that infamous island prison for enemies of the British Empire, St Helena.

There was to be one last desperate struggle against the realities of defeat. It began not in Zululand but in Natal in 1906 where, ironically, the reality of colonial control, of taxation and forced labour, of removal from the land and the erosion of traditional forms of authority, had been experienced over a longer period and never tested by arms. It was a movement that nostalgically harked back to the days of the old Zulu order, and sought to draw on the power of the imagery of the old Zulu kings by evoking royalist war cries and by the choice of King Cetshwayo's grave as a rallying point. It was ruthlessly put down by colonial troops armed with Maxim machine guns and quick-firing artillery in a campaign which has little trace of the glamour which still attaches in the popular imagination to the war of 1879, but which reveals the naked truth of the common processes underlying both.

The British

Allan, William Wilson VC

William Allan (the surname is often given as Allen) was born in Northumbria to Scottish parents in 1844 and joined the Army in York on 27 October 1859 being posted a few days later to the 2nd Battalion 24th Regiment.

His early career was typical of many Victorian 'other rankers' in that he was confined to the cells for alcohol-related offences on several occasions, but by the early 1870s he seems to have made a determined effort to improve himself. While at the depot in Brecon in 1874 he assisted in the regimental school; he was appointed lance corporal in 1876 and corporal in 1877.

In 1876 he married Sarah Ann Reeves and the couple subsequently had eight children. In 1878 he was awarded a prize for good shooting and distance judging. He was posted to B Company, 2/24th, from the depot shortly before the battalion was sent to the Cape to take part in the closing stages of the 9th Cape Frontier War. B Company took part in the skirmishing around the Xhosa strongholds of Intaba-ka-Ndoda and the Perie Bush. At the end of 1878 the battalion was attached to the No. 3 (Centre) Column for the invasion of Zululand. When the Column crossed into Zululand at Rorke's Drift on 11 January 1879 B Company was left to guard the Drift and supply depot which had been established in the mission buildings. Shortly after noon on 22 January the Column was attacked and the camp at Isandlwana overrun; at about 4.30

p.m. elements from the Zulu reserve crossed the Mzinyathi River and attacked the post at Rorke's Drift. Allan was among a number of good shots who seem to have been deliberately selected to hold the rear wall of the post, facing Shiyane hill. This barricade was the subject of the first Zulu rush, but the attack was halted at fifty yards' range. A fire-fight then developed between the men manning the rear wall and Zulus occupying the rocky terraces at the foot of Shiyane. In the course of this Allan was hit in the upper arm by a musket-ball as he leaned on the barricade to fire. His wound was bound up and he then distributed ammunition to the rest of the defenders. Allan was among the first group recommended by Lieutenant Bromhead for the Victoria Cross and the award was gazetted on 2 May 1879.

Allan's injury was such that he was invalided home in August 1879. He was treated at Netley hospital and received his award from Queen Victoria at Windsor Castle on 9 December 1879. He was promoted sergeant while still with the 2/24th. He settled in Monmouth and, despite the lasting effects of his injury he transferred to the 3rd (Militia) Battalion, South Wales Borderers, in October 1881. He was appointed colour sergeant and later instructor of musketry with first the 3rd and later the 4th Militia Battalions. In 1890, however, he fell victim to an influenza epidemic and, after several weeks of illness, he died on 12 March. He was buried with military honours in Monmouth cemetery.

Barrow, Major Percy

Percy Henry Stanley Barrow was born in 1848, educated at Cheltenham and entered the 19th Hussars as a cornet in 1868. He was promoted to the rank of lieutenant in 1870, and in January 1875 he became captain and Commandant of the School of Instruction for Auxiliary Cavalry. In 1877 he was given the position of Brigade Major of Cavalry at the Curragh. Sir John French – who served under him in the Sudan – described him as:

The finest and best character I ever met. He was small in stature, spare and light. I think he had the reddest head of hair I ever saw on any man. His face was expressive of power and intelligence.

Barrow volunteered as a 'special service' officer in response to Lord Chelmsford's request before the outbreak of the Zulu campaign. He was given command of No. 2 Squadron, Mounted Infantry, which was attached to Colonel Pearson's column, and then command of all the column's mounted troops. From the moment the column crossed the border, he was active in scouting the lines of advance and harassing Zulu scouts. On 22 January he was present in the action at Nyezane. Following the occupation of Eshowe and the news a few days later that the Centre Column had been defeated at Isandlwana, Pearson decided to send his mounted men back to the border because of the difficulty of corralling and feeding the horses. Barrow duly returned to the Thukela on 28 January. Here he patrolled the border until Lord Chelmsford was able to assemble a column to march to the relief of Eshowe. Barrow was then attached to this column as commander of mounted troops. He took part in the Battle of kwaGingindlovu on 2 April, where he was wounded in the leg – possibly hit by a spear as he stood on a wagon watching the fight. In the closing stages of the battle he led the mounted men in a determined and ruthless pursuit of the demoralized Zulu army. Barrow's men accompanied Lord Chelmsford's flying column in the relief of Eshowe, and on 4 April spearheaded an attack on Prince Dabulamanzi's eZulwini homestead.

After the Eshowe campaign Barrow commanded the mounted men attached to the 1st Division and was given the post of Assistant Adjutant General. He returned to England at the end of the war and in 1880 was appointed ADC to the Aldershot Division. In 1881 he returned briefly to southern Africa during the closing stages of the Transvaal Rebellion. He returned to Aldershot as brigade major but joined Sir Garnet Wolseley's 1882 expedition to Egypt, again commanding mounted infantry. In 1883 he was promoted lieutenant colonel. In 1884 he commanded his own regiment, the 19th Hussars, in the fighting against the Sudanese Mahdists around the Red Sea port of Suakin. At the Battle of El Teb on 29 February his horse was killed and he was surrounded by Mahdists warriors. One of his men, Quartermaster Sergeant William Marshall, dashed to rescue him, and in doing so earned the Victoria Cross; Barrow, however, received a number of wounds, the effects of which would eventually kill him. He died in Cairo on 13 January 1886.

Beresford, Lord William VC

William Leslie de la Poer Beresford was born in Mullachbrach, Markethill, County Armagh, Ireland, on 20 July 1847. He was the third of five sons of John de la Poer Beresford, who was then recorder of Mullachbrach but later succeeded his brother as Marquess of Waterford in 1859. Beresford was educated at Eton where an early reference to his 'turbulent disposition' hinted at boisterousness and aggressive temperament that would stay with him throughout life. After a period studying French and German in Bonn he entered the 9th Lancers as a cornet in June 1867. He was ideally suited to cavalry life being a great lover of horses and dogs; he was a member of the regimental polo team, established a racehorse stud at Epsom, and enjoyed steeple chasing. In 1870 he was promoted lieutenant and in 1874 sailed to India as an ADC to the Viceroy, where he served in the Afridi expedition of 1874. In 1876 he was promoted captain. With the outbreak of the 2nd Afghan War he requested permission to return to his regiment which was on active service, taking part in the fighting around Ali Musjid. When news of Isandlwana reached India, Beresford applied for six months' leave to join the fighting. He arrived in Natal in April 1879 and soon earned the nickname 'Fighting Bill', a reference not merely towards his soldierly capabilities but to his willingness to settle points of honour with his fists. He was appointed a staff officer to Colonel Redvers Buller, and took part in the advance on oNdini.

On 3 July Beresford accompanied Buller's reconnaissance across the White Mfolozi River. Buller's troops were led into a skilfully executed ambush by Zulus under the command of *inkosi* Zibhebhu kaMaphitha, and only Buller's intuition prevented them from being surrounded. During a hasty withdrawal towards the river, a Sergeant Fitzmaurice of the Mounted Infantry was unhorsed, and Beresford turned to help him. Fitzmaurice was stunned by the fall and by his horse rolling on him, and at first did not heed Beresford's urgings until he famously shouted 'Come along, you bloody fool. If you don't I'll punch your bloody head for you!' As Fitzmaurice struggled to climb up behind Beresford, Sergeant O'Toole of the Frontier Light Horse came to their assistance, holding the Zulus back with his revolver.

Beresford and Fitzmaurice reached the White Mfolozi safely; Beresford's back covered with blood from Fitzmaurice's bleeding nose. As they crossed the river, they passed the war correspondent of *The Graphic*, Charles Fripp, who was in the act of sketching the skirmishing and was later to paint a famous painting of Isandlwana. As the troops withdrew, Fripp was left isolated and Buller sent him a curt order to withdraw; Fripp, not knowing from whom the order had come, made a dismissive remark in Beresford's hearing. Beresford promptly dismounted and threatened to 'thrash' Fripp; the two squared up to one another on the river bank, Zulu bullets still splashing nearby, until Fripp's fellow correspondents dragged him away.

Beresford was present inside the square during the Battle of Ulundi the following day. He was later awarded the Victoria Cross for his part in Fitzmaurice's rescue, which was presented to him by Queen Victoria at Windsor Castle after his return to England.

Beresford then returned to India and his position as ADC to the Viceroy. In December 1884 he was promoted major and he took part in the 3rd Burma War (1886-1887). He was appointed brevet lieutenant colonel in July 1887 and lieutenant colonel in 1890. In 1894 he was placed on half-pay and returned to England where he met and married Lilian Price, whom he married in April 1895. He spent much of his retirement in a country house near Dorking, indulging his love of horses. In 1896 he had a serious riding accident in which he broke his pelvis. His health declined and he died as a result of peritonitis on 28 December 1900.

Blood, Bindon

Bindon Blood was born on 7 November 1842, the eldest son of Mr W.B. Blood of County Clare, Ireland. Bindon was directly descended from Colonel Thomas Blood who, in 1671, had attempted to steal the Crown Jewels from the Tower of London. He was educated in Ireland and passed into the East India Company training college at Addiscombe (which produced officers for the East India Company's army). Addiscombe was amalgamated shortly afterwards into the Royal Military Academy at Woolwich, and when Blood passed out he was gazetted into the Royal Engineers in December 1860. In 1871 he was sent to India and worked initially in the Public Works Department in Bombay and then with the Bombay Sappers and Miners. He was promoted captain in 1873 and saw his first action on the North-West Frontier expedition in 1877-78. In 1879 he was sent to Natal to command the 30th Field Company RE as part of the reinforcements dispatched after Isandlwana. He was attached to Major General H. H. Crealock's 1st Division and appointed its commander of Engineers. He was responsible for building the pontoon bridge across the Lower Thukela River using a system he had designed himself. He emerged from the war a brevet major and returned to India to take part in the 2nd Afghan War.

On his return to England in 1882 he was given command of 26th Field Company RE, which was sent to join the Egyptian campaign. He was present at the decisive Battle of Tel-el-Kebir and was promoted brevet lieutenant colonel. He returned to India, where he spent much of his later career.

In 1883 he married Charlotte Colvin, the daughter of a distinguished Indian and Egyptian administrator. He commanded the Bengal Sappers and Miners and was promoted lieutenant colonel (1888) and full colonel (1893). Physically fit, active and energetic he enjoyed polo, pig-sticking and hunting; his 'bag' of tigers apparently ran to an apocalyptic fifty-seven. He was heavily involved in the North-West Frontier campaigns of the 1890s, as chief of staff on the Chitral Relief expedition and then commander (1897) of the Malakand and Swat expeditions. At this time he had as an ADC Lieutenant Winston Churchill of the 4th Hussars. In 1898 he was given command of the Meerut District and promoted major general, and in 1901 he was sent to southern Africa again to take part in the Anglo-Boer War. He commanded a district in the Transvaal and led a mobile column. In October 1901 he returned to India to command the Punjab (Northern District). He was promoted lieutenant general in 1902 and full general in 1906. He retired in November 1907 and was awarded the GCB in 1909. In retirement he took an interest in the business world and on the outbreak of the First World War he devoted his energies to recruitment. From 1914 he was Colonel Commandant, Royal Engineers, and when, in 1936, the ancient office of Chief Royal Engineer was revived, Blood was awarded the position. In 1933 he published his autobiography, *Four Score Years and Ten*. He died in London on 16 May 1940 at the decidedly ripe old age of ninety-seven.

Bonaparte, Prince Napoleon Eugene Louis Jean Joseph

Louis Napoleon Bonaparte, as he was generally known, was born at the Tuilieries Palace, Paris, on 16 March 1856. His father was Louis Napoleon III, Emperor of the French, and his mother a minor noblewoman, Eugenie de Montijo,the illegitimate daughter of George Villiers, 4th Earl of Clarendon, later British Foreign Secretary who, at the time of Eugenie's conception, was having an intense affair with her married mother.

Louis was the grandnephew of the great Napoleon Bonaparte. In the aftermath of the Anglo-Prussian victory at Waterloo in 1815 the Bonaparte family had gone into hiding in

Europe. Napoleon's only son and heir, Napoleon Francois, given the title King of Rome, had lived most of his life a virtual prisoner of the Austrian royal court and had died in 1832; it fell to Napoleon's nephew, Louis Napoleon (senior) to take up the cause of Bonapartism. Louis Napoleon had tried, and failed, to intervene in French politics several times before securing a place in the government on the back of the revolution of 1848 which finally ousted the French monarchy and established a republic. In 1851 Louis Napoleon had staged a coup d'etat, overthrown the elected government and declared himself Emperor. He took the title Napoleon III in deference to the late King of Rome. His son Louis, whose birth offered the prospect of a permanent Bonaparte dynasty, was given the title Prince Imperial.

The Prince grew up in a claustrophobic environment, smothered by his loving parents and inculcated with the glory of the Bonaparte name. He was photographed in military uniform as an infant and paraded before the French public dressed as a soldier. He had no possible future but that of Emperor Napoleon IV but his aspirations were cut short when, in 1870, France was defeated by the emerging Prussian power of Otto von Bismarck. Napoleon III manfully tried to marshal his armies himself but proved lacking in the spectacular talents of his uncle; he was captured by the Prussians. A popular uprising in Paris, a reaction to military defeat, chased the Empress Eugenie and her son out of France. They took refuge across the Channel in England where the Emperor, released by the Prussians, later joined them. Although the British Government was uncomfortable at Britain playing host to the descendants of Britain's greatest military enemy of recent times, Queen Victoria was sympathetic to their plight. The Imperial family rented a mansion at Chiselhurst in Kent.

The defeat of 1870 had come as a severe shock to Louis whose faith in his destiny as a Bonaparte had been severely damaged. He became withdrawn and introverted. In 1872 an English friend suggested that he be allowed to train as an officer at the Royal Military Academy at Woolwich. While

28

there was no possibility that Louis – as a potential foreign head of state – could ever serve as a British officer he took up the post and delighted in the study of the military profession. Although an individualist, and unaccustomed to the team spirit which pervaded the culture of his fellow cadets, he proved popular and hard working.

On 9 January 1873, Napoleon III died. In the eyes of Bonapartist supporters his son Louis, the Prince Imperial, became the Emperor Napoleon IV in waiting. After his graduation in 1875, Louis was given an honorary attachment to a Royal Artillery garrison battery and took part in summer manoeuvres but for the most part his life entered a limbo, awaiting a call to lead his countrymen, which was unlikely, in fact, ever to come. He looked for an opportunity to volunteer for active service in a European conflict in order to establish his reputation as a soldier but the possible political repercussions prevented him.

In February 1879, the news of Isandlwana reached England. Several of Louis' artillery friends had already secured special service posts in Zululand and Louis determined to follow their example. The war had little potential political risk as few people in Europe cared about the fate of the Zulus; at first Louis' mother, the Empress Eugenie, was appalled at the idea. He talked her round, however, and she in turn secured Queen Victoria's support. Louis was given permission to sail to Zululand as an observer with no official rank. He did, however, wear his Royal Artillery uniform from the moment of his departure. He took with him a note from the Commander-in-Chief, the Duke of Cambridge, asking Lord Chelmsford to find him a useful post.

Louis arrived in Durban at the beginning of April, a few days after Lord Chelmsford's victory at kwaGingindlovu. He was attached to Chelmsford's staff as an ADC. Almost immediately Louis displayed symptoms of an unspecified illness, possibly tick-bite fever, from which he never, in the time left to him, fully recovered. As Lord Chelmsford moved his headquarters north to the Zulu border, to supervise the assembly of the 2nd Division. Louis was attached to the staff of Colonel Richard Harrison, Acting Quarter-Master General, who was busy planning routes for the imminent invasion. In the middle of May Louis accompanied several long-distance patrols into the Zulu border country to search for viable roads. On these occasions he displayed an unnerving lack of discipline, being anxious to prove himself in personal combat with Zulu scouts and risking the safety of the patrols in consequence. As a result of objections raised by Colonel Redvers Buller, Harrison was directed to confine Louis to deskwork. He spent the last half of May copying maps and drawing up reports.

The advance of the 2nd Division was scheduled for 1 June. By that time, the country ahead had been repeatedly swept by British patrols and was believed to be free of hostile forces. Louis asked permission to take a patrol ahead of the advancing column to verify camping routes and Harrison – probably out of sympathy for Louis' frustration – agreed. There is no evidence that the patrol had any necessary military objectives. The Prince was to be escorted by six men of an irregular unit, Bettington's Horse, and six mounted auxiliaries, and accompanied by a Zulu guide. A member of the headquarters staff, Lieutenant J. Brenton Carey asked for, and was granted, permission to accompany the patrol.

The patrol left the 2nd Division camp at Thelezeni early on 1 June. The mounted auxiliaries had failed to make the rendezvous and the patrol consisted of Bettington's men alone. Despite his lack of official standing the Prince, who was in uniform and riding a white horse he called Tommy, which he had bought in Durban, issued commands throughout. The patrol passed several miles ahead of the cavalry screen in front of the advancing column and halted on a hill looking down into the Itshotshozi River valley. The valley appeared to be deserted and Louis suggested the patrol descend to a deserted Zulu homestead before returning. Here the patrol halted, the men made coffee, and the Prince – who was apparently still unwell – dozed in the shade. At about 4.15 p.m. the Zulu scout

30

indicated that he had seen a Zulu moving through the long grass nearby. Carey woke the Prince who insisted on waiting a few more minutes; the horses were then gathered and the Prince gave the order 'Prepare to Mount!' As he gave the command 'Mount' a ragged volley broke from the long grass and mealies surrounding the homestead.

A scouting party of between fifty and seventy Zulus of various *amabutho* had been watching the patrol since it had descended into the valley. The Zulus had advanced under cover of the banks of the Itshotshozi and had almost surrounded the homestead when they saw the patrol prepare to mount. The burst of gunfire frightened the horses and the patrol scattered. Those who were securely in the saddle galloped away; two troopers, Abel and Rogers, were killed. The Zulu scout escaped on foot but was later overtaken and killed. Louis had one hand on the holsters at the front of his saddle when the firing began; he tried to jump up but his horse pulled away, following the others. Louis, still holding the saddle, ran alongside until they reached a donga about fifty yards away. Here the horse lurched, the strap between the holsters tore and Louis fell. The horse kicked him as it struggled free. Winded, Louis turned to find several Zulus in close pursuit. His sword had fallen from its scabbard and he tried to hold the warriors away with his revolver, but his shots missed. He ran into the donga. He was hit by a thrown spear, which he pulled out and brandished at his attackers but, stepping backwards, he put his foot in a hole and stumbled. The Zulus closed in and speared him to death.

Lieutenant Carey was not aware of the Prince's death until the prince's riderless horse overtook him. Carey and the survivors rode on to the nearest British camp and reported the incident. A strong cavalry patrol was sent out the following day to recover the bodies. Abel and Rogers were found near the homestead and buried where they fell; Louis' body was found in the donga. He had been stripped in accordance with Zulu ritual and his stomach lightly cut. He bore no less than nineteen distinct spear wounds (two of which were officially described as exit wounds to avoid any suggestion he had died with his back to the enemy; in fact, of course, he had been surrounded).

A funeral service was held at Thelezeni that day but Louis' body was roughly embalmed – the entrails removed and the body salted – and sent down the line of communication to be shipped to England. Each stage of the journey was accomplished with great ceremony, and at Pietermaritzburg and Durban the cortège was paraded through the streets. The body was then shipped back to England where it arrived on 10 July. In circumstances very nearly approaching a state funeral it was interred in the Catholic chapel at Chiselhurst.

Lieutenant Carey was later tried by court martial for misbehaviour before the enemy in connection with the incident. At the end of the war efforts were successfully made to recover Louis' bloodied uniform which was returned to his mother

In May 1880 the Empress Eugenie made a pilgrimage to the Itshotshozi River and spent the anniversary of his death in a midnight vigil on the spot where he was killed. She later bought Farnborough Abbey, in Hampshire, and built a mausoleum to contain the bodies of both Napoleon III and the Prince Imperial; the remains were transferred in 1888.

The Prince's death caused a scandal in both Britain and France where the Republican government, hitherto a political enemy, discovered a sudden nostalgic sympathy for him. Whether he would ever have become Emperor is impossible to say; given the events of the late nineteenth and early twentieth centuries in Europe, however, it seems unlikely.

The Empress Eugenie lived to see the fall of Imperial Germany and died in 1920.

Booth, Anthony Clarke VC

Anthony Clarke Booth was born on 21 April 1846 in the village of Carrington, near Nottingham. In 1864 he attempted to join the Royal Marine Light Infantry, but was refused because of a heart murmur. In October 1864 he was accepted into the 80th Regiment, however. He joined the regiment in its depot in County Cork, Ireland, where he met his future wife, Lucy O'Brien. The couple would, in due course, have eight children. From 1864 until 1872 Booth's service was in England, but in 1872 the 80th was sent to Hong Kong, sailing from there to southern Africa in 1877. On the outbreak of the Anglo-Zulu War, the 80th was attached to Colonel Rowland's No. 5 Column, and several companies were detached to protect the exposed frontier settlement of Lüneburg. On 7 March a company-sized detachment under Captain David Moriarty was dispatched from Lüneburg to escort an overdue convoy of eighteen wagons carrying supplies. Moriarty located the wagons but had difficulties in crossing the flooded Ntombe River, close to Lüneburg. For several days his command was split, with wagons on either side of the river, and subject to poor weather conditions. On the night of 11-12 March, Booth – then a sergeant – was on the southern bank with a detachment commanded by Lieutenant Henry Harward, while a larger contingent, commanded by Moriarty himself, was on the northern bank. Just before dawn on the 12th, some 800 Zulus under the command of Prince Mbilini waMswati attacked the stranded convoy. The position on the north bank was soon overrun and large numbers of warriors crossed to attack Harward's party. According to Booth's own account:

> I commanded the party on this side as Lieutenant Harward saddled his horse and galloped away leaving us to do the best we could, when I saw all our men across, about fifteen in number and all as naked as they was born, I sent them on in front and we retired firing ... there was hundreds of [Zulus] crossing the river to try and cut us off but we made good our escape to a mission station and expected to be outflanked there but we fought our way to within a mile of Lüneburg.

Booth was promoted to colour sergeant the day following the attack in recognition of his gallantry, and was later awarded the Victoria Cross. He was presented with the award by Queen

Victoria at Windsor Castle on 26 June 1880, after the 80th had returned to Ireland.

Booth served in the Army for a total of 33 years and 182 days, spending many of his later years as a sergeant instructor in Lichfield, Staffordshire. He retired in April 1898, but shortly afterwards suffered an attack of rheumatic fever. He died on 8 December 1899.

Bourne, Frank

Frank Bourne was the son of a farmer and born in Balcomb, Sussex, on 27 April 1855. He enlisted in the Army at Reigate, Surrey, in December 1872. He was posted to the 1st Battalion 24th Regiment, number 1961, and later transferred to the 2nd Battalion 24th Regiment in January 1873. He rose rapidly to become colour sergeant of B Company on 27 April 1878, when the battalion was in South Africa. So far from being the mature man of popular myth he was just twenty-five at the time of the action at Rorke's Drift and, because of his youth, was known to his men as 'the kid'. That he had achieved a senior NCO rank at such an early age is indicative, however, of his steadiness and efficiency. He was the senior sergeant in B Company during the Battle of Rorke's Drift on 22-23 January and was awarded the Distinguished Conduct Medal for his gallantry. He was also offered a commission but refused because he did not have the private income to support it. After the war he continued to serve with the 24th – later the South Wales Borderers – for a total of seventeen years. He was appointed Sergeant Instructor of Musketry in July 1880 and in 1890 he was made quartermaster and honorary lieutenant. He retired in 1907 but volunteered for service on the outbreak of the First World War and served as a musketry instructor; he retired as honorary lieutenant colonel in 1918. He was awarded the OBE for his First World War services.

In September 1882 he married Eliza Fincham in Bombay and the couple had five children. Bourne remained proud of the part he had played at Rorke's Drift – 'I considered myself lucky to have been there' – and commemorated the battle with a dinner on the anniversary each year, although he discouraged his family from discussing it otherwise. He was one of the longest surviving veterans of the battle and died in Dorking, Surrey, on 9 May 1945, having lived long enough to witness the defeat of Hitler's Germany.

Bromhead, Gonville VC

Gonville Bromhead was born at Versailles, France, on 29 August 1845. He was one of the four sons of Edmund de Gonville Bromhead of Thurlby Hall, Lincolnshire, and his wife Judith. His was a distinguished military family; his father had fought as a lieutenant with the 54th Regiment at Waterloo, where he lost an eye, and at the storming of Cambrai. His grandfather was a lieutenant general who had fought in the American Revolutionary War and been captured at Saratoga; his great-grandfather served as an ensign under Wolfe at Quebec in 1759. Gonville's elder brother had fought in the Crimea, and another brother was killed in the 2nd Afghan War. Gonville's younger brother Charles was an officer in the 24th Regiment.

Gonville was educated at Thomas Magnus School in Newark-on-Trent where he developed a life-long passion for cricket and other physical sports including boxing. He entered the 24th Regiment as ensign by purchase on 20 April 1867. He became a lieutenant in 1871. He was very much a regimental officer, comfortable with his colleagues in the mess but awkward and uneasy with strangers. His retiring personality may have been due to a hearing problem, which was a common enough ailment among Victorian soldiers.

In January 1878 he was a subaltern attached to B Company when the 2nd Battalion was ordered to the Cape. It arrived in time to take part in the later stages of the Cape Frontier War and Bromhead was present at a number of skirmishes in the bush. When his immediate senior, Captain Alfred Godwin-Austen was wounded, apparently by accident, Bromhead assumed command of B Company, with whom he was apparently a popular officer. In late 1878 the 2/24th was ordered to join its sister battalion as part of the Centre Column assembling on the Helpmekaar heights for the invasion of Zululand. On 11 January 1879 the column crossed into Zululand at Rorke's Drift and on the 20th both battalions accompanied the forward move to Isandlwana. Bromhead and B Company were left to guard the supply depot at Rorke's Drift. This was a routine duty; there is not the slightest evidence that B Company was selected because of Bromhead's deafness, or any other reason

Early on the afternoon of the 22nd, the first survivors from the disaster at Isandlwana streamed past the post. Bromhead was junior to Lieutenant Chard RE, who was working on the ponts by the river, and sent to inform him; in the meantime Bromhead made preparations for defence or, should Chard prefer, retreat. When Chard came up he discussed the matter with Bromhead and Assistant Commissary Dalton and it was agreed to fight. The stacks of supplies at the post were hastily dragged out to fortify the buildings. At about 4.30 p.m. about 3,500 Zulus arrived and began a piecemeal attack on the fortifications. Bromhead played a prominent part in managing the defence under Chard's orders and joined in the hand-to-hand fighting where necessary. At one point during the night, he commanded a vulnerable sector between the biscuit-box partition and the front barricade where most of the men around him were shot down. When the Zulu attacks died down, Chard and Bromhead stood on the barricades listening for the sounds of Zulu movements in the dark. By dawn the next morning the battle was over and Chard and Bromhead celebrated by sharing a bottle of beer which was found in a ransacked Engineers' wagon.

Bromhead was awarded the Victoria Cross for his gallantry in May 1879. He was promoted captain and brevet major but he was not temperamentally suited to the fame his heroism brought him. He was reluctant to discuss the battle and left no long written report of it. He was presented with the award by Sir Garnet Wolseley on 11 September 1879 at Utrecht. Wolseley, typically, formed an uncharitable impression of him

– he declared of Chard and Bromhead that 'two duller, more stupid, more uninteresting even or less like gentlemen it has not been my luck to meet for a long time'. In September 1879 the 2nd Battalion sailed to Gibraltar; Bromhead took the opportunity to return briefly to the UK where he was invited to an audience with Queen Victoria. He rejoined his battalion in India, and his last years were spent between Britain and India. He was present during the 3rd Burma War of 1886 but died of enteric fever (typhoid) at Camp Dabhuara, Allahabad, India, on 9 February 1892.

Gonville's younger brother, brevet Major Charles James Bromhead, served with the 2/24th in Zululand from February 1879 and commanded burial expeditions to Isandlwana in September 1879.

Browne, Edward Stevenson VC

Browne was born in Cambridge on 23 December 1852, the son of Salwey Browne and his wife Elizabeth. Salwey Browne was then a student; he later served as an officer in the 68th Regiment. Browne passed through Sandhurst and was commissioned as an ensign into the 1st Battalion 24th Regiment in September 1871. He was promoted to lieutenant the following month. He served with the battalion in Malta, Gibraltar and at the Cape. He took part in the Griqualand West expedition of 1875 and in April 1877 was part of a detachment of the 1/24th formed into the 1st Squadron, Imperial Mounted Infantry. The squadron was widely employed throughout 1877 and 1878 providing an escort of Theophilus Shepstone in the Transvaal, taking part in the 9th Frontier War and Sir Hugh Rowlands' 1878 Sekhukhune expedition. On the outbreak of the Anglo-Zulu War, the 1st Squadron was attached to the Centre Column. On 11 January, the day of the invasion, it escorted Lord Chelmsford to a rendezvous with Colonel Wood; the following day it took part in the attack on *inkosi* Sihayo's homestead. On 21 January, as a prelude to a general movement of the Column, Lieutenant Browne and a patrol of just four mounted men scouted towards the Siphezi Mountain; they withdrew after light skirmishing with Zulu patrols, not realizing that they had come close to intercepting the movement of the main Zulu army from Siphezi to the Ngwebeni valley. The following morning the squadron left the camp at Isandlwana as part of Lord Chelmsford's command and spent the day skirmishing in the Mangeni hills.

In the aftermath of Isandlwana, Browne and the 1st Squadron were re-allocated to Colonel Wood's column. On 28 March they formed part of Lieutenant Colonel John Cecil Russell's detachment which attempted to assault the western end of the Hlobane mountain complex. Russell decided that the steep pass connecting the lower plateau of Ntendeka with the main mountain was impractical for mounted men, and so did not proceed; he sent Browne and a few Mounted Infantry up the pass to inform Colonel Buller's party of the decision. Browne remained on Hlobane until Buller's troops arrived and began to descend the pass under heavy attack. The following day, when Wood's camp at Khambula came under attack from the main Zulu army, the 1st Squadron formed part of the mounted foray which stung the Zulu right into an unsupported attack. According to an eyewitness:

> One of his own troopers, a private of the 2nd Battalion 4th King's Own, got dismounted and was so confused at his stumble that he would certainly have been sacrificed, as the Zulus were close upon him. Lieutenant Brown [e] helped the man to mount, thus saving his trooper's life at imminent risk of his own.

Browne was later awarded the Victoria Cross for his gallantry (the citation incorrectly gives the date as 28 March, which has led to some confusion that the incident in fact took place at Hlobane). Browne continued to serve with the squadron throughout the campaign; he took part in the skirmish on the White Mfolozi on 3 July and was present at the final Battle of Ulundi on 4 July.

After the war Browne was promoted captain in May 1880

and major in November 1885. From 1881 to 1886 he was adjutant of the 3rd Battalion, Monmouthshire Rifle Volunteers (South Wales Borderers) and in 1891 he served in India as the Deputy Acting Assistant Adjutant General, Musketry, in Bengal. He was promoted lieutenant colonel in 1893 and colonel in 1897. That year he became commanding officer of the 24th Regimental District in Brecon. His last years were spent on home service commands and he retired in November 1906 with the rank of brigadier general and a CB. He died at Montreaux, Switzerland, on 16 July 1907 aged fifty-four.

Buller, Redvers Henry VC

The son of James Wentworth Buller, a Devonshire squire and sometime MP, Redvers (a West of England name apparently pronounced 'Reevers') was born at the Buller family seat of Downes, near Crediton, in 1839. He was educated at Eton and his family purchased him a commission in the 60th Rifles in 1858. He served in India and China and took part in Sir Garnet Wolseley's 'Red River' expedition in Canada in 1870 against the mixed-race Metis people. Wolseley's judgement of Buller's character reveals the characteristics that dominated his early career – 'full of resource and personality and personally absolutely fearless, those serving under him always trusted him fully'. When Wolseley prepared for his expedition against the Asante in West Africa three years later he appointed Buller his chief intelligence officer. After the campaign Buller returned to the UK with the rank of major and spent four years in the adjutant general's department. In 1878, however, he sailed to the Cape to take part in the 9th Frontier War. Here he was employed raising and commanding irregular cavalry, a task to which he proved extremely adept. According to George Mossop, a trooper in the Frontier Light Horse:

> Tough and brusque he was, but his troopers discovered that he was both accessible and sympathetic. If we were lying in the rain, so was Buller. If we were hungry, so was he. All of the hardships he shared equally with his men. Never did

Buller, as commander, have a patrol tent to sleep under whilst his men were in the open. He was the idol of us all.

With the outbreak of the Anglo-Zulu War, Buller was appointed to the command of the irregular cavalry troops attached to Colonel Wood's column with the rank of lieutenant colonel. He and Wood made a formidable team; confidant of each other's judgement, equally dynamic, and wary of outsiders. Portraits of Buller at the time suggest something of his strength of character and restless energy in his piercing eyes, gaunt features and heavy beard. On campaign he was apt to fight in a practical civilian Norfolk jacket and wide-brimmed hat. Buller was responsible for extensive sweeps through the northern border districts on the outbreak of the war, and for the capture of the abaQulusi stronghold at Zungwini Mountain on 20 January. He constantly took the war to the enemy, raiding and burning the royal homestead at abaQulusi, destroying Zulu homes in retaliation for Zulu counter-attacks and carrying away Zulu cattle. In the aftermath of the Zulu attack on the 80th Regiment's convoy at Ntombe on 12 March Buller raided the homesteads of *inkosi* Manyanyoba Khubeka in the Ntombe valley.

On 28 March Buller led one of the assault parties which attempted to storm the Hlobane Mountain. Bivouacking out in the field the night before, he moved his camp after dark, leaving campfires burning at the old site so as to deceive the enemy. He personally led his column onto the summit through abaQulusi musket fire at first light. Once up, he attempted to secure the summit and rounded up large numbers of Zulu cattle grazing there. His men came under heavy pressure from the abaQulusi, who cut the lines of retreat and gradually drove Buller across the summit. The arrival of a large Zulu army from the direction of oNdini meant that Buller's command had to descend as quickly as possible. Their only way off the mountain was a rugged staircase of rock later known as the Devil's Pass. During the descent the retreat became a rout as Zulus harassed the British troops on all sides. Buller personal-

40

ly rescued several men who had lagged behind or lost their horses and who would have been killed by the Zulus – an act for which he received the Victoria Cross. That night, as the survivors of his command struggled back to Wood's camp at Khambula, Buller searched for stragglers in the dark. The following morning, when the Zulu army attacked Khambula, Buller led a sortie of mounted men, which provoked the Zulu right 'horn' into launching an unsupported attack – an action that was largely responsible for the British victory. During the pursuit, in the final stages of the battle, Buller led his men out again after the retreating Zulus and appeared, in one memorable phrase, 'like a tiger drunk with blood'.

Buller continued to command the mounted troops under Wood during the latter stages of the war. In May, when Lord Chelmsford was assembling reinforcements on the border, Buller commanded a number of long-range patrols into Zululand in search of a viable invasion route. When the invasion began his men screened the advance. On 5 June they encountered Zulu resistance in the hills above the uPoko (Ntinini) stream; they were withdrawn and replaced by the 17th Lancers, who promptly lost their adjutant, Lieutenant Frith, to a Zulu sniper in the action. On 3 July Buller commanded a foray across the White Mfolozi River to select a spot near the oNdini homestead for Lord Chelmsford to fight a battle. The foray was ambushed by Zulus commanded by Zibhebhu kaMaphitha but Buller's instinctive reaction prevented his men from falling into a worse trap and he got most of them safely back across the river. On 4 July Buller was present at the Battle of Ulundi, and his mounted men again took a ruthless part in the pursuit of the defeated Zulu Army.

Buller and Wood returned to the UK at the end of the war and were received by Queen Victoria. The Queen observed:

Colonel Buller is reserved and shy, with rather a dry, gruff manner. He also, though naturally averse to talking, told me much that was very interesting. He is very downright when he does speak and gives a very direct answer... .

Colonel Buller is very modest about himself, saying he had
got far too much praise.

Buller returned to Natal in 1882 as Wood's chief of staff at the
end of the Transvaal Rebellion. They arrived too late to take
part in the fighting but Buller met many of the Boer leaders,
reinforcing an opinion formed in Zululand that the Boers were
by no means an insignificant military force. Buller returned to
Downes and in August 1882 married a widow, Lady Audrey
Howard, a marriage which brought him four stepchildren. The
couple later had a daughter of their own. In 1882 Buller went
to Egypt as Wolseley's head of intelligence staff during the
Urabist campaign. He was rewarded with a KCMG. In 1884
he was appointed chief of staff to Sir Gerald Graham's expedition to defend the Red Sea port of Suakin against the
Mahdist movement and fought at El Teb and Tamai. On his
return to England, still only forty-four, he was made a major
general. The following year he accompanied Wolseley again
during the unsuccessful Gordon Relief Expedition and was
given command of the desert column after Sir Herbert Stewart
was wounded. He defeated a Mahdist attempt to halt the
column at the Battle of Abu Klea (16-17 February 1885). The
expedition was a failure, however, and Buller returned to
England. In 1886 he served in a civilian capacity in unsettled
Ireland – where his Liberal sympathies were inclined to
support the Irish tenants rather than the interests of the landed
gentry – and in 1887 he was appointed Quartermaster-
General. From 1890 to 1897 he occupied the key position of
adjutant general, based at Aldershot, and he embarked on a
programme of reform of the British Army. In 1896 he was
promoted full general.

With the outbreak of the Anglo-Boer War in October 1899
Buller was given command of an Army Corps and sent to the
front. It was an appointment he had been reluctant to accept;
he was now sixty and felt himself too old. His physical appearance had changed from the wiry man of his youth and he was
heavy and bloated, his face almost a caricature of a peppery

general. Nevertheless, the Queen herself placed great trust in him and he was hugely popular with the British public. When he arrived at the Cape he decided to direct his main effort to the relief of the beleaguered town of Ladysmith. Here he faced very real strategic difficulties, for the Boers were well emplaced in positions above the formidable Thukela River. Buller's undoubted concern for his men, and the respect he felt for the Boers, led to a tentative attack on the position at Colenso on 15 December, which soon ground to a halt. Buller shifted the emphasis of his attack and probed Boer positions close to Spioenkop upstream. An attack on Spioenkop itself was defeated on 23-24 January.

By now Buller – who had never enjoyed a good relationship with the press – was coming under severe criticism for his failings, although he still enjoyed the confidence of his men. After a failed attack at Vaalkranz he finally managed to break the Boer lines in a series of actions along the Thukela heights at the end of February. Ladysmith was relieved and Buller followed up the retreating Boer forces, driving them back through the Kahlamba Mountains. Nevertheless, his poor press image and his difficult working relationship with his colleague, Lord Roberts – whose son had been killed at Colenso – led to London recalling Buller in October 1900. Stung by criticisms of his conduct of the war, Buller made an impromptu speech at a luncheon in London in October 1901 in which he attempted to justify his actions. His remarks were held to be a breach of discipline, and he was placed on half-pay a few days later. His career was effectively over and he spent his last years at Downes, the decades of exemplary service largely undermined by his failure against the Boers. He remained popular with the public at large and died on 2 June 1908.

Campbell, the Hon. Ronald George Elidor

Ronald Campbell was born on 30 December 1848, the second son of the Earl of Cawdor and his wife Sarah. He was educated at Eton and entered the Army in 1867 as an ensign in the

Coldstream Guards. In 1871 he was promoted lieutenant and then captain and was appointed adjutant, a post which he only relinquished in October 1878. In 1872 he married Katherine, the daughter of Bishop Claughton. Campbell volunteered for service in southern Africa and on his arrival in Natal was appointed Staff Officer to Colonel Wood. Campbell was an energetic and hard-working officer and established a good relationship with Wood. He was present during most of Wood's skirmishes in Zululand from the time No. 4 Column crossed the Ncome River on 6 January.

On 28 March Wood assaulted the Hlobane mountain complex. The actual attack was left to assault parties, but Wood and his staff came close to the scene of operations to observe. Early that morning they encountered a detachment of Irregulars, Weatherley's Horse, skirmishing with Zulu riflemen close under the cliffs on the southern flank of the mountain. The exact details of the events that followed remain controversial, largely because they have been traditionally dominated by Wood's version of events. A Zulu marksman seriously wounded Wood's interpreter, a civilian named Llewellwyn Lloyd, and Wood's own horse was killed. Campbell and Wood's ADC, Lieutenant Lysons, carried Lloyd's body a short way down the hill when, according to Wood, he then ordered Weatherley's men to clear the Zulu snipers from among the rocks – but they refused. According to Wood, Campbell snapped 'Damn him! He's a coward!' Campbell ran forward calling out 'I'll turn them out', and Wood ordered his personal escort forward in support.

A recently published account by Captain Dennison, a surviving officer of Weatherley's Horse, suggests that the Irregulars were fully engaged and that Wood's order was a reckless one, born of impatience or bravado. In either case, Campbell rushed into a crevice between the fallen boulders and, according to one witness, 'his helmet flew off and [he] fell dead with the top of his head blown off' by a musket shot at close range. The Zulus were driven from the crevices and Campbell's body was brought down beside Lloyd's. Wood insisted that a handful of auxiliaries accompanying him dig a grave with their spears, and he personally read the burial service.

Wood was much upset by the death of both Campbell and Lloyd, and retired from the Hlobane battlefield.

In May 1880 the Empress Eugenie undertook a pilgrimage to Zululand on the anniversary of his death to attend the spot where her son, the Prince Imperial, had been killed. Evelyn Wood commanded her escort, and Campbell's widow secured permission to accompany the Empress as a lady-in-waiting. The expedition made the journey via Hlobane, where Wood had several of his own ghosts to lay to rest. A granite cross, made by a stonemason in Pietermaritzburg, was carried up the mountainside and, in Katherine's presence, placed on the spot where Campbell and Lloyd lay buried. The bearers were local Zulus recruited on the day, many of whom had fought in the battle.

The visit brought a sense of closure to Katherine Campbell who was deeply moved by the awesome scenery of the battle-field. Sadly, this grave – one of the loneliest of those left by the British Army in Zululand – has been repeatedly vandalized in the years since.

Carey, Jahleel Brenton

Jahleel Brenton Carey was born at Burbage, Leicestershire, in July 1847, the son of a country parson, Adolphus Carey (later vicar of Brixham in Devon). Carey inherited his impressive biblical name from his maternal grandfather, Sir Jahleel Brenton, who had distinguished himself as a commander of a frigate during the Napoleonic Wars (like many Victorians, Carey seems to have preferred his middle name, and signed himself 'J. Brenton Carey'). Carey spent much of his youth in France, and was educated at French schools. He then entered Sandhurst to train as an officer in the British Army and in 1865 took a commission in the 3rd West India Regiment, a colonial unit maintained by the Crown for work in the Caribbean and West Africa. Such regiments were unpopular in fashionable Army circles, and Carey's choice was probably dictated by a lack of funds; it was generally accepted that Colonial regiments allowed officers to enjoy a moderate standard of living at far less cost than their Line counterparts. Carey was stationed in both Jamaica and West Africa, and found himself at one point the senior commander of a British fort at Accra, on the Gold Coast of Africa, at the age of twenty; even by Victorian standards, when junior officers were routinely given testing responsibilities, this was unusual, and suggests that his superiors had great confidence in Carey's abilities. In 1867 Carey saw his first taste of action in a campaign against the Indians of British Honduras. In a campaign that was marked by mismanagement and setbacks, Carey emerged with a commendation for his efficiency and thoroughness.

In 1870, however, the 3rd West India Regiment was disbanded, and Carey placed on half-pay. This was a blow to an ambitious officer with few influential friends to help his career, the more so since that year, on 25 May, Carey had married Annie Isabella Vine of Jamaica. The outbreak of the Franco-Prussian War offered him a way forward. The war – which was seen by theorists in England to offer a clash between two very different European military traditions – was keenly studied by the British Army, and many young officers sought excuses to see something of the fighting. Carey, with his knowledge of French, joined the English Ambulance Service. He emerged with a commendation of thanks and a 'cross and ribbon' for his help to the French wounded, and at about that time purchased an exchange into a Line Regiment, the 81st. He then transferred to the 98th, which was stationed in his old haunts, the West Indies. He seems to have made a good impression – he was appointed Garrison Adjutant – and in 1878 he was accepted into the Staff College.

Contrary to the opinions expressed after the Zulu campaign, Carey seems to have been a bright, ambitious and very thorough officer, about whom no doubts had hitherto been expressed on the question of his personal courage. There was, in fact, little that was unusual about the European influences of his youth and, in his oft-quoted religious conviction and open devotion to his family, he was no more than part of a mainstream pattern of belief among Army officers at the time.

When news of the British defeat at Isandlwana reached England, Carey volunteered for a 'special service' staff post. He was accepted, and set sail on the steamship *Clyde*, which was carrying replacement drafts for the ill-fated 1/24th, at the beginning of March. The *Clyde* reached Simon's Bay safely and refuelled in excellent time, but in the early hours of 3 April, as she rounded the southern tip of the African continent, she struck a reef a mile from Dyer Island. She was holed and began sinking, but not quickly, and there was plenty of time to organize an orderly evacuation. Carey was given command of one of the first two boats to be put ashore, and he was later commended for the thorough way in which he prepared an improvised bivouac on land.

Carey and the 1/24th drafts were duly rescued from the Cape sands and arrived in Durban a few days later. At first, it seemed that Carey might be given a post with the 1st Division, already massing on the coast, but instead he accompanied the 1/24th drafts on their march to Dundee, where the 2nd Division was assembling. Carey arrived there on 4 May, and a few days later was attached to the staff of the Acting Quarter Master General, Colonel Richard Harrison, as his deputy.

Carey's duties consisted of assisting Harrison in the planning of the projected invasion route of the 2nd Division. It was at this time that Carey first met another of Harrison's staff, Prince Louis Napoleon Bonaparte, the exiled heir to the Imperial throne in France.

Although much has been written of the close friendship which sprang up between Carey and Louis, it is almost certainly exaggerated. Carey's fluent French certainly attracted Louis, and there is no doubt the two got on well; but when they first met Louis had less than three weeks to live, and he spent very little of it in Carey's company. The two were assigned different duties and only went on one patrol together before the fateful 1 June, and messed separately – Carey with Harrison and Louis with Lord Chelmsford's staff.

On 18 May both Carey and Louis joined Harrison in a long-range patrol through Zululand, looking for a viable road for the column. Although the border districts were largely deserted by the Zulus, the patrol was engaged in at least one skirmish. It is interesting to note that no doubts were expressed at the time about Carey's conduct; only after 1 June was it hinted that he had been a nervous participant.

At the end of the month Carey was involved in another incident which became controversial after the event. At Lord Chelmsford's insistence, he rode out to sketch the line of advance, escorted by a squadron of the 1st Dragoon Guards. This later earned him a rebuke from the officers of the Cavalry Brigade, attached to the 2nd Division; but the object of their irritation was not that Carey had insisted on an entire squadron as escort (he had not), but that Lord Chelmsford had seen fit to employ regular cavalry on such work without consulting the senior Brigade officers.

The general advance of the 2nd Division was scheduled for 1 June. The previous night Louis begged to be allowed to patrol ahead once it had begun. In fact, the first few miles beyond the border had been swept clear of Zulus, patrolled and sketched many times, but Harrison, sympathetic to Louis' sense of frustration and desire to be at the head of the army, agreed. As an afterthought Carey asked, and was given, permission to accompany the patrol to verify his existing sketches.

Louis and Carey left the British camp at dawn the following morning. They were escorted by six men from an Irregular unit, Bettington's Horse, and an African scout, and were supposed to be joined by a party of African auxiliaries, but in the confusion of the advance these were missed. As they rode out, the patrol passed several groups of scouts and officers, including one of Chelmsford's staff. Although he held no rank, Louis issued the commands, and Carey went along with them.

The patrol advanced several miles beyond the protective screen in front of the column, and at Louis's suggestion

48

descended into the valley of the Itshotshozi River to rest at a deserted Zulu homestead. Louis – who had recently been ill – seemed tired, and Carey let him rest. Then, shortly before 4 p.m. the African scout reported that he had seen a Zulu in mealie fields nearby. The Prince gave the order to mount, but as they did so a volley broke out from the long grass around the homestead. The patrol had been spotted by a Zulu scouting party, and almost surrounded. Startled by the close range volley the patrol's horses scattered in confusion, riding across a donga less than 100 yards away. Only some distance beyond the donga did Carey attempt to take stock; four men were missing, including the African scout, and Prince Louis Napoleon.

Carey returned to break the news of Louis' apparent death that night, and the following morning led a large cavalry detachment to find the body. It became evident that, in those first few seconds when they were caught by surprise and out-numbered, everyone in the patrol – including the Prince – had run. Carey now found himself the subject of whispered accusations of cowardice. Most of these originated not from his own 2nd Division colleagues, but from the officers of Wood's Flying Column. A number of Louis' friends were on Wood's staff, and Wood seems to have allowed the rumours to spread unchecked as a means of distancing himself from the embarrassment caused to Lord Chelmsford by the incident.

On 4 June, at Carey's request, a Court of Inquiry was convened to investigate the circumstances of the incident. Carey had hoped that it would clear him of any misconduct, but in fact it recommended he be tried by court martial on a charge of misbehaviour before the enemy.

The court convened on 12 June. Carey defended himself, and the survivors of the skirmish appeared as witnesses. Crucial to Carey's defence was the question of command, and he insisted that throughout Louis had issued the orders. Although survivors confirmed this, the fact that Louis held no official rank counted against Carey. He was found guilty. Contrary to popular belief, however, he was not sentenced to be cashiered, and in fact the court made no recommendation regarding a sentence. They were clearly sympathetic to Carey's predicament, and indeed hinted that the removal of his staff post might be sufficient punishment enough. Lord Chelmsford refused to decide a punishment either, and Carey was ordered to return to England to await the decision of higher authorities.

By the time he reached Plymouth on 20 August, Carey's public position had radically altered. Here he learned that he had been promoted to captain – which had been approved before the incident of 1 June – and that a sizable section of the British public, fearing he had been made a scapegoat, had risen to his defence. He learned, too, that owing to a technicality in the way the records of the court martial had failed to reflect whether the leading officers had been sworn in, the Judge Advocate General had set the findings aside. Carey was free to return to his regiment.

At this point, however, his misplayed his hand. Caught up in the enthusiasm for his vindication, he sought reconciliation with Louis' mother, the Empress Eugenie. Eugenie, however, thought Carey entirely to blame and the idea tasteless, and used her influence with Queen Victoria to isolate Carey. Snubbed, he returned to his regiment, his promising career in tatters, his reputation the subject of strong and divided feelings among his fellow officers.

By 1882 the 98th was on garrison duty in India. Here, at Karachi on 22 February 1883, Captain Jahleel Brenton Carey died of peritonitis. Of the many legends that surround him, the last – that he was kicked to death by a white horse, similar to the one the Prince Imperial had been riding on 1 June 1879 – is, like much of the rest said about him, without foundation.

Chard, John Rouse Merriott VC

Chard was born at Boxhill, near Plymouth, Devon, on 21 December 1847, the son of William Wheaton Chard and his wife Jane. Chard was one of three sons and four daughters; his elder brother Wheaton joined the Army and his younger brother, Charles, the Church.

Chard was educated at Plymouth New Grammar School and the Royal Military Academy, Woolwich. He passed out in 1868 and was commissioned as a lieutenant in the Corps of Royal Engineers.

After two years' training at Chatham he was sent to Bermuda in October 1870 were he was employed building fortifications. After a spell of similar service in Malta, he returned to England.

Towards the end of 1878 Lord Chelmsford requested that Royal Engineer companies be dispatched to southern Africa, and despite their misgivings about the looming Zulu crisis the Government agreed. The 2nd and 5th Companies RE were selected, and Chard was attached as an extra subaltern to the 5th Company, commanded by Captain Walter Jones. The company sailed for the Cape on 2 December 1878 and arrived at Durban on 5 January. It was directed to join the No. 3 (Centre Column) but the weather conditions were so poor that the company was greatly delayed on the road. Lord Chelmsford, who was preparing to advance deeper into Zululand, sent a special request for an officer and a detachment of Sappers to be hurried forward to ease the transport difficulties in his immediate rear. Chard was given the job and arrived at Rorke's Drift on 19 January. His detachment camped by the river, where they found the flat-bottomed ponts in need of repair after the heavy traffic of the invasion. They remained there when the column moved forward to Isandlwana the following day. On the 22nd, however, Chard received an order that his Sappers were required at the forward camp. Uncertain whether his own services were required he accompanied them, but, on discovering he was needed at the river, he returned to Rorke's Drift. He reported to the senior officer there, Major Spalding, that there were Zulu movements close to Isandlwana, and Spalding decided to ride to Helpmekaar, some twelve miles distant, to hurry forward a company of infantry who were supposedly camped there. Before he left he casually examined an Army List, which gives officers' seniority by date of commission and promotion, and observed that Chard would be in command during his absence. With no Sappers to command, Chard passed the afternoon quietly writing letters to his family when, shortly after 3 p.m. his attention was attracted to two men riding hard on the other side of the river. He sent the pont across for them, and they proved to be survivors of the disaster at Isandlwana.

Chard reported to the nearby mission station where he found the small garrison was already making preparations for defence. Consulting with Lieutenant Bromhead – commanding a company of the 2/24th, Surgeon Reynolds and the commissariat officers, Chard agreed that defence offered the best hope of survival. A stockpile of supplies was dragged out of one of the mission buildings and hastily formed into barricades; Chard – the Engineer – selected the lines of defence. They were scarcely completed when, about 4.30 p.m. some 3,500 Zulus, who had crossed the border in the aftermath of their victory at Isandlwana, came into view. They began to assault Chard's defences in a battle that was to last throughout the night. The British garrison was driven out of one of the mission buildings, which was set on fire, and only escaped annihilation by their desperate stand in front of the other building. Before dawn the Zulus withdrew.

Although there is clear evidence that the Zulu incursion was no more than a disorganized border raid, the successful defence of Rorke's Drift offered the British a huge morale boost in the aftermath of Isandlwana and allowed Lord Chelmsford to claim that a Zulu attack on Natal had been repulsed. Eleven of the defenders of Rorke's Drift were awarded the Victoria Cross, and Chard was one of the first to be nominated.

In recent times it has become fashionable to underplay Chard's contribution to the defence, citing his lacklustre early career as proof of his lack of imagination. It is certainly true that General Sir Garnet Wolseley, in presenting the award to Chard in the field on 15 July 1879, commented that 'a more uninteresting or more stupid-looking fellow I never saw', and

Chard's lack of dash as a company officer was certainly noted by his senior, Captain Jones. But if Chard genuinely seems to have possessed a relaxed and rather genial personality, unblighted by an excess of initiative, the command skills he displayed on the day were exemplary. From the layout of the interior barricades – which prevented the defensive perimeter from unravelling, as one area after another fell to the Zulus – to his unfaltering and inspiring determination to resist, Chard's contribution to the defence was critical. The Battle of Rorke's Drift was nothing if not a test of character, and John Chard was not found wanting.

The strain of the battle took its toll on Chard's health and, like many of the Centre Column survivors cooped up in the insanitary conditions at the mission after the battle Chard succumbed to disease. He was sent to Ladysmith to recover. When he recovered he rejoined the 5th Company, which was by then attached to the 2nd Division, and was advancing upon oNdini. He had been promoted captain and then brevet major in recognition of his gallantry immediately after the battle. The advance was not without its risks, even to the hero of Rorke's Drift. The advance was plagued by false alarms at night and, during one particularly bad scare at Fort Newdigate on the night of 6-7 June, Chard and a party of Sappers – who were working on the fortifications and had pitched their tents outside the main camp – were mistaken for the enemy. They were compelled to huddle in a ditch as the infantry poured volley after volley over their heads until the error was discovered.

It was during the advance on oNdini that Chard seems to have earned the dislike of Colonel Evelyn Wood, and much of the damage done to Chard's reputation can be laid at Wood's door. In his memoirs, Wood, while mentioning no names, recalls an incident in which he castigated a 'lazy' officer whom he caught one day, as a wagon train was about to become entangled in a difficult drift, 'sitting with his back to them smoking, apparently quite unconcerned'. This officer, who 'belonged to another Corps', was Chard; a dynamic individual himself, Wood had no time for more plodding dispositions, and was undoubtedly irked by Chard's sudden celebrity. It was Wood who shaped Wolseley's assessment of Chard – 'Wood tells me he is a most useless officer, fit for nothing' – and Wood again who belittled his appearance before Queen Victoria.

Yet Chard seems unaware of the jealousies he had provoked, and served with his company to the end of the war. The 5th Company was present among Lord Chelmsford's troops who crossed the White Mfolozi River on 4 July, and from inside the square Chard witnessed the Zulu army dash itself to pieces one final time on the massed firepower of the regular infantry.

At the end of the war, in October 1879, Chard returned to England to be feted as a popular hero, to receive a succession of presentations, of swords of honour and addresses and invitations to dinner receptions. Shortly after he arrived he was invited to an audience with Queen Victoria; whatever Wood may have said about his looks, the Queen liked his unassuming manner, and he was invited back again four months later. He posed for his own portrait in at least two famous paintings of the battle.

His later military career offered little to compare with Rorke's Drift, and it is unlikely that he expected it might. He served in peacetime garrisons at Devonport, in Cyprus and in Singapore. He was promoted major in July 1886, lieutenant colonel in January 1893 and full colonel in January 1897. In 1896 he returned to the UK to command the Royal Engineers in the Perth District. That autumn, however, he was diagnosed as suffering from cancer of the tongue, the result no doubt of his life-long passion for his pipe. Several operations failed to halt the progress of the disease and in August 1897 he went on the sick list. Queen Victoria wrote to express her concern. Chard moved in with his brother Charles, who was vicar of the village of Hatch Beauchamp in Somerset, and here he died on 1 November 1897, aged forty-nine.

Chelmsford, General Lord

Frederic Augustus Thesiger was born on 31 May 1827 (he

succeeded to the title Lord Chelmsford on 5 October 1878). His grandfather, John Andrew Thesiger was born in Dresden, a Saxon gentleman who emigrated to England and became secretary to an influential English statesman. Thesiger's father, also Frederic, was a lawyer and a Tory MP who became Lord High Chancellor of England and was ennobled as the first Baron Chelmsford. The first Baron married Anna Maria Tinling in 1822 and had four sons and three daughters, of whom Frederic was the eldest. Frederic's background, although the family was not rich, was conventional for a Victorian gentleman. His education at Eton was followed by the purchase of a commission, initially into the Rifle Brigade, and then into the Grenadier Guards. He was a conscientious and diligent officer at a time when most officers did not take much interest in their military duties. He was subsequently promoted to the rank of captain and appointed ADC to the commander of forces in Ireland. In 1855 he joined his regiment in the Crimea and thus missed the Battle of Inkerman, in which the Guards played so crucial a role. He was designated to a succession of staff duties and ended his posting to the Crimea as Deputy Assistant Quartermaster General.

A further promotion brought him the lieutenant colonelcy of the 95th Regiment and it was with his new regiment that he sailed for India in 1858. By the time they arrived the Indian Mutiny had all but been suppressed but they were involved in mopping-up operations in Central India during 1859. Chelmsford's reputation as a competent staff officer resulted in his appointment as Deputy Adjutant General.

When General Sir Robert Napier was ordered to mount an expedition against King Theodore of Abyssinia in 1868, he chose Chelmsford to be his Deputy Adjutant General. In a well-organized and successful expedition, the Anglo-Indian force suffered few casualties despite the potential for disaster. Chelmsford emerged from the campaign with much credit, being mentioned in dispatches and being made Companion of the Bath for his tireless staff work. He was also appointed ADC to the Queen and made Adjutant General of India. This period of his life was to be his happiest and most successful, for in 1861 he married Adria Heath, the daughter of an Indian Army general, who eventually bore him four sons. It was also at this time that he became friendly with the Governor of Bombay, Sir Henry Bartle Frere, a man who would have considerable influence on Chelmsford's subsequent life. After sixteen years service in India, Chelmsford was recalled home. With little in the way of family wealth, the prospect of expensive entertaining befitting an officer of his rank was a constant source of worry to him.

When he was offered the post of Deputy Adjutant General at Horse Guards, he felt obliged to decline and made known his wish to take a command again in India, where the cost of living was much cheaper. Instead, he was promoted to brigadier general commanding the 1st Infantry Division at Aldershot pending a suitable overseas posting.

It was fate that the vacancy he accepted occurred in South Africa and was, coincidentally, his first independent active service command in thirty-four years. He was able to renew his association with Sir Bartle Frere, now the High Commissioner for South Africa, and to share Frere's vision of a confederation of southern African states under British control.

When Chelmsford arrived at the Cape in February 1878 the fighting against the Xhosa was entering its final stages. His subsequent experiences against a foe that relied on hit-and-run tactics, rather than becoming involved in a full-scale battle, coloured his opinion of the fighting capabilities of black Africans. Chelmsford did, however, show himself to be a commander who did not shirk hard work, often riding great distances over rugged country in the effort to break any remaining resistance. He was a commanding figure with his tall, spare frame, pleasant features, usually hidden by a black beard and bushy eyebrows. His manner was quiet and polite and he had the impeccable manners of a Victorian gentleman. Although the Cape Frontier campaign had left him wary of the capabilities of colonial officers he seldom let his frustration show and was generally held in high regard. He had shown himself to be a traditionalist of the old school, however, reluctant to delegate authority and preferring to trust a handful of subordinates with whom he was comfortable rather than establish a trained staff. As a tactician he had proved competent but uninspired.

With the successful conclusion of the Frontier War Chelmsford followed Frere's political agenda for the invasion of Zululand. He had initially planned to invade Zululand in five columns but a lack of resources forced him to reduce this to three offensive and two defensive columns. He decided to accompany the Centre Column in person, a decision which effectively deprived the designated commander, Colonel Glyn, of a meaningful role. He also failed to address the friction which developed between his own staff and Glyn's.

Chelmsford crossed the border on 11 January. On the 12th he attacked and destroyed the stronghold of the border *inkosi* Sihayo kaXongo. Because of the poor state of the roads he delayed advancing to his next objective, Isandlwana, until the 20th. No sooner had he arrived here than he personally rode out to scout the Mangeni hills for signs of a Zulu presence.

Although he was later criticized for not placing the camp at Isandlwana on a defensive footing, he argued that he had not intended it to be permanent and indeed was already planning to advance by the 22nd.

That plan was interrupted by the discovery of a Zulu force at Mangeni on the evening of the 21st. Receiving the report in the early hours of the 22nd, Chelmsford decided to split his command and move to support his reconnaissance. Although this decision was much criticized, it was made in accordance with the best intelligence available at the time and was an attempt to seize the initiative. Unfortunately, as a result, Chelmsford spent most of 22 January skirmishing in the hills twelve miles from Isandlwana, while the Zulus attacked and carried the camp in his rear.

In the aftermath of the disaster Chelmsford kept his emotions firmly under control. The enormity of the events nearly crushed him, for he had no confidant to whom he could unburden his feelings. He wrote to his wife but her support and sympathy took many weeks to reach him. He fluctuated between confidence and despair and contemplated resigning. Adding to Chelmsford's woes were the relentless personal attacks on him by the newspapers which further eroded his confidence. His friends advised him to retire on health grounds but, with Wood's decisive victory at Khambula and the arrival of several regiments of Imperial troops, Chelmsford seemed to sufficiently recover his determination to defeat the Zulus. He personally chose to lead the column to relieve Colonel Pearson's besieged force at Eshowe. At Gingindlovu, Chelmsford and his staff had displayed the Victorian officers' disdain of enemy fire by remaining standing to encourage the troops, many of whom were newly arrived raw recruits. The result of such foolhardy exposure was that, although Chelmsford was not hit, among his staff Crealock was slightly wounded in the arm and lost his horse, while Captain Molyneux had two horses killed.

With Eshowe relieved, Chelmsford was able to plan a fresh invasion of Zululand. He reorganized his troops to form two main thrusts. The 1st Division, comprising Pearson's old command and reinforcements from home, would advance up the coast. Two further columns, acting in tandem so as in effect to be one, – the newly constituted 2nd Division and Wood's column, now called the Flying Column – would advance from the central border. Chelmsford decided to accompany the 2nd Division and thereby exercised control over this sector of the advance. As his forces and supplies built up, so Chelmsford's confidence appeared to return. Once the invasion was under way, he moved cautiously, laagering his camp every night, building forts to protect his lines of communication and scouting well ahead. Nevertheless, it was on one of these map-making reconnaissances that another misfortune befell the luckless commander. During a routine reconnaissance by a small patrol, which included the Prince Louis Napoleon, a group of Zulus opened fire on the party and in the scramble to safety, two troopers were shot from their horses and the Prince was caught and slain. When the news broke in the British newspapers, the shock was even greater than that of the Isandlwana massacre. Chelmsford could not reasonably be blamed for the Prince's death but, following all the previous disasters, his culpability was implied.

Towards the end of June Chelmsford was informed that Sir Garnet Wolseley was being sent to Zululand to supersede him. The reasons stated were not that Chelmsford had failed as a field commander but that the strain of the war effort had brought the relationship between the Army and the colonial authorities in Natal to breaking point. Although this was a personal blow, it redoubled Chelmsford's determination to vindicate his reputation by a victory in the field before he was replaced. In the event it was a close-run thing. Wolseley arrived just too late to prevent Chelmsford disobeying his previous direct order not to attack Cetshwayo. Chelmsford proceeded to inflict a crushing defeat on the Zulus at Ulundi on 4 July, which allowed him to hand over his command on a high note.

Chelmsford then resigned his command immediately. He sailed home on the RMS *German* in the company of Wood and Buller, his most effective and reliable commanders.

He found opinion about his performance divided at home. The Prime Minister, Disraeli refused to receive the commander who had cost the country so much and brought discredit to the Government. Some newspapers continued to pillory Chelmsford, popular songs mocked him and even some of his fellow peers were critical. But the military establishment rallied to his support and he enjoyed the continued confidence of the Commander-in-Chief, the Duke of Cambridge, and Queen Victoria herself.

Chelmsford was showered with honours. His rank of lieutenant general was confirmed and the Queen used her influence to have him appointed Lieutenant of the Tower and later Gold Stick. He later became a full general and Colonel of the Sherwood Foresters and then of the 2nd Life Guards. Edward VII made the ageing general a GCVO. He was not, however, entrusted with a field command again.

On 9 April 1905, at the age of seventy-eight, Lord Chelmsford had a seizure and died while playing billiards at the United Service Club. So died a man with many admirable attributes but who was thrust into a position for which he was not intellectually equipped. He is largely remembered today as the man ultimately responsible for the Victorian Army's greatest military defeat.

Clery, Cornelius Francis

Francis Clery – as he preferred to be called – was born in Ireland in 1838 and educated at Dublin and Sandhurst before he joined the 32nd Regiment as an ensign at the age of twenty in 1858. He was promoted lieutenant in 1859 and captain in 1866. In 1868 he entered the Staff College, a move which deepened his interest in the academic aspects of soldiering. He passed out in 1870 and took up a post as instructor – later professor – of tactics at Sandhurst. In 1875 he wrote a handbook on 'minor tactics' which was to remain a standard for twenty years despite his own lack of front-line experience. He served on the staffs of Ireland and Aldershot before sailing to the Cape in 1878 as a special staff officer with the rank of major. He served briefly in the Griqualand West and 1878 Sekhukhune expeditions before being appointed to the Zululand invasion force. Clery hoped to secure the post of staff officer to Colonel Wood but when that went to Captain Campbell he instead took up the job of principle staff officer to Colonel Glyn of the Centre Column.

Lord Chelmsford's decision to accompany that column effectively deprived Glyn – and his staff – of a real purpose, and Clery complained that there was little to do beyond the most mundane column duties. It was Clery who marked out the position of the camp at Isandlwana when the column arrived there on 20 January. A good deal of tension existed between Glyn's staff and that of Lord Chelmsford, and in particular Clery disliked Chelmsford's assistant military secretary, Lieutenant Colonel Crealock. Like Crealock, Clery himself also had a sharp tongue and an acerbic pen. Clery was with

Glyn during the skirmishing of 22 January at Mangeni and in the aftermath of the Isandlwana disaster sought to shield Glyn from attempts by Chelmsford's staff to make him a scapegoat. Following Captain Campbell's death at the Battle of Hlobane on 28 March, Clery was transferred to Wood's column as staff officer and deputy acting adjutant. He served with Wood's column throughout the war and was present at the Battle of Ulundi on 4 July. Clery returned home in August 1879. In 1882 he served in the Egyptian campaign as Assistant Adjutant and Quartermaster General, and in 1884 he served under General Sir Gerald Graham as a brigade major in the fighting against the Mahdists around the Red Sea port of Suakin. His *Times* obituary gives an interesting insight into his style of personal leadership:

> Sir G. Graham's force was almost the first to be uniformed in khaki, but Clery, a military dandy of the old school and influenced more honourably by his conception of the duty of a staff officer to be easily seen, clung to his red tunic, and to it owed, incidentally, praise as high as has ever been accorded by a general to a subordinate. At the hard-fought and dangerous Battles of El Teb and Tamai the scarlet-clad Clery was everywhere, and everywhere conspicuous; and General Graham recorded that 'when at any critical period I saw his red coat, I knew that there matters would be going well, or, if wrong, would soon be rectified, and turned my attention to another part of the field'.

Clery received the CB for his Sudanese service and was promoted brigadier general. He remained in Egypt until 1887 when he returned to England as Commandant of the Staff College. He was promoted to major general in 1894 and given command of a brigade in Aldershot. With the outbreak of the Anglo-Boer War in 1899 Clery was given command of a division with the rank of lieutenant general. His senior officer was his old Anglo-Zulu War colleague, Redvers Buller. Clery was nominally given charge of the troops sent to Natal to relieve Ladysmith but ironically Buller's decision to accompany that detachment himself effectively robbed Clery of his command – much as Lord Chelmsford had done to Glyn twenty years before. Clery, by now elderly, cautious and vain enough to dye his greying side-whiskers, allowed his strategy to be dictated by Buller with disastrous results at Colenso on 15 December 1899. And Clery's reputation suffered along with Buller's. After Ladysmith was finally relieved, Clery was allotted the task of protecting the lines of communication. He left southern Africa in October 1900 with a KCMG but retired from the Army in February 1901. He died in 1926.

Clifford, Henry Hugh VC

Clifford was born on 12 September 1826 and entered the Army as an ensign in the Rifle Brigade in 1846. In 1847 his regiment was sent to southern Africa to take part in the 7th Cape Frontier War, and indeed Clifford was also present during the 8th War (1852-1854). He was still a lieutenant when the regiment was sent to the Crimean War. During the Battle of Inkerman on 5 November 1854 Clifford led a rush into the confused mêlée, killing one Russian with his sword, disabling another and saving the life of a soldier. For his gallantry he was awarded the Victoria Cross. He was promoted captain in 1854, major in 1855 and lieutenant colonel in 1858. He served in the China expedition and was assistant quartermaster general in Aldershot from 1860 to 1864 and at the war office from 1865 to 1868. He was appointed ADC to the Duke of Cambridge. He was promoted colonel in 1864 and major general in 1869. He was one of four major generals sent out to assist Lord Chelmsford in the aftermath of Isandlwana. Because of his administrative experience the Duke of Cambridge suggested that he was made inspector general of forces in Natal and on the lines of communication. In fact, however, the tortuous supply situation brought Clifford into conflict with Chelmsford and Clifford resented the fact that his authority stopped at the border, which, he claimed, made efficient management of transport resources impossible.

After the war Clifford was King Cetshwayo's gaoler at Cape Castle. In 1880 he was briefly administrator of the Transvaal and on his return to England he was appointed commander of the eastern District. He died on 12 April 1883.

Cochrane, William Francis Dundonald

Cochrane was born in Corsham, Wiltshire, on 7 August 1847, the son of Colonel W. M. Cochrane and his wife Mary. The Cochranes were a distinguished military and naval family – William's great-uncle was the Lord Cochrane who rose to prominence in the Navy during the Napoleonic Wars, and went on to play a significant part in the independence struggles in South America – and it was perhaps inevitable that William should join the forces. He was educated at Kensington School and Sandhurst. He entered the 32nd Light Infantry as an ensign in 1866. He purchased a commission as a lieutenant in 1868, and was adjutant of his regiment from 1870 until 1878. During the 1870s the 32nd was employed on garrison duty at the Cape but returned to the UK shortly before the outbreak of the last Cape Frontier War (1877-78).

In 1878 Cochrane volunteered to return to the Cape as a 'special service' officer for the pending invasion of Zululand. On the ship out, one of his companions, Lieutenant Henry Harford, commented on Cochrane's lively personality, observing that he 'was simply the life and soul of the ship, always ready to sit down at the piano and sing a good song, or get up concerts, theatricals and other amusements'. On his arrival Cochrane was appointed Transport Officer to Colonel Durnford's No. 2 Column. This column, originally based at Middle Drift, was moved up to Rorke's Drift to support Lord Chelmsford's forward movement to Isandlwana. On the 22nd, Durnford was ordered forward to Isandlwana, and Cochrane was party to the discussions concerning the command of the camp, and to Durnford's decision to ride out with his own command to sweep the iNyoni escarpment. Cochrane described how Durnford's command 'proceeded between five and six miles' at a canter before encountering the Zulu left advancing in the opposite direction. Cochrane was present during Durnford's stand in the bed of the Nyogane stream and retreated with them to the camp when they were driven out. Here he 'saw that all was over', and rode off after the retreating survivors. He crossed the Mzinyathi at Sothondose's Drift and made his way to Helpmekaar. In later years he was fond of saying that he escaped 'by damn all but the ears of my horse'.

With the reorganization of the African auxiliary forces, which followed Isandlwana, Cochrane was given command of the Natal Native Horse with the rank of captain and attached to Colonel Wood's Left Flank Column. He was present as part of Colonel J.C. Russell's command during the aborted assault on Hlobane mountain on 28 March, and at the Battle of Khambula the following day, where many of the NNH refused to retire inside the British laager but harried the Zulu right 'horn' from a distance instead. The NNH was subsequently heavily involved in the advance of the Flying Column to oNdini, and Cochrane took part in the Battle of Ulundi on 4 July. The NNH began the battle by provoking the Zulu attacks, and then retired inside the British square, later emerging to take part in the ruthless pursuit.

At the end of the war Cochrane was appointed Assistant Adjutant-General to the Colonial Forces at the Cape, and as such took part in the BaSotho 'Gun War' (1880-1881). He was promoted captain in June 1881 and brevet major in February 1882. In 1882 he returned to regular service and took part in Sir Garnet Wolseley's Egyptian expedition. A series of staff appointments – in Hong Kong, Ireland and South Africa – followed. In 1886 he was promoted major.

In 1893 he married a Chilean woman, Maria Carola. The same year he was given a brevet lieutenant-colonelcy and offered command of a brigade of troops in the Anglo-Egyptian Army. He held this command for several years during the slow preparations for the British 're-conquest' of the Sudan. During the advance to Omdurman in 1898 he held a command on the line of communications. He left the Sudan with a CB and a colonelcy, and his last postings were in Belfast.

He retired in September 1903 with the honorary rank of brigadier general. He died on 23 October 1927.

Coghill, Nevill Josiah Aylmer VC

Coghill was born on 25 January 1852 in Dublin, the eldest son of Sir John Jocelyn Coghill of Drumcondra, County Dublin. He was educated at Haileybury then served two years in the Dublin Militia before entering Sandhurst and obtaining a commission in the 1st Battalion, 24th Regiment in February 1873. He served in Gibraltar and the Cape where he was appointed ADC to General Sir Arthur Cunynghame. He remained on Cunynghame's staff throughout the early stages of the 9th Cape Frontier War and returned to England when Cunynghame was replaced by Lieutenant General Thesiger (Lord Chelmsford). He returned to Natal to join the preparations for the invasion of Zululand and was appointed ADC to Sir Bartle Frere. Being anxious to join his battalion for the campaign he received permission to serve on Colonel Glyn's staff as an ADC and hurried to the front to join the invasion. He was at Glyn's side during the attack on Sihayo's homestead on 12 January and on 20 January he accompanied the staff on a patrol to the Mangeni gorge. This patrol made Lord Chelmsford decide to sweep the surrounding heights the following day; on his way back, however, Coghill exuberantly set off on horseback chasing after a chicken, fell, and further damaged his knee which was recovering after some earlier horseplay in the mess. As a result he did not accompany Chelmsford's column on the morning of the 22nd when it set out from Isandlwana to reinforce Major Dartnell's command at Mangeni.

Coghill's role in the subsequent battle at Isandlwana went largely unrecorded, although his knee probably prevented him from taking an active part. Once the line collapsed he left the camp and was spotted riding through the Manzinyama valley before he joined Lieutenant Melvill. The two attempted, independently, to cross the swollen Mzinyathi at Sothondose's (later Fugitives') Drift and Coghill got out safely on the Natal bank; Melvill, however, was unhorsed and clung to a large rock midstream, where he was joined by an NNC officer, Lieutenant Higginson. Coghill saw their plight and put his horse back into the water but it was immediately hit by a Zulu bullet and killed. Coghill swam to Melvill and Higginson and the three assisted each other across the river. The Colour was, however, lost. They climbed up the steep hills on the Natal bank – slowly, because of Coghill's injury – until Higginson left them to look for horses. Shortly afterwards Melvill and Coghill were overtaken and killed.

Their bodies were discovered by a patrol from Rorke's Drift on 4 February. The Colour was discovered in the riverbed. Melvill and Coghill were buried where they fell but were later exhumed and reburied a few yards away beneath a conspicuous rock. Sir Bartle Frere paid for a stone cross to be erected at the site. There was no provision for the posthumous award of the Victoria Cross in 1879, and it was merely announced that Melvill and Coghill would have received it 'had they survived'. Coghill's father, Sir John Coghill, lobbied on his late son's behalf, and in 1906 the rules were changed to allow for posthumous awards. In 1907 Coghill was awarded the Victoria Cross retrospectively; his attempted rescue of Melvill was cited in the award.

In 1973 Melvill and Coghill's graves were vandalized and Frere's cross damaged. It was removed from the site for twenty years but has recently been replaced at the head of the grave.

Colley, George Pomeroy

Colley was the third and youngest son of the Hon. George Francis Colley and his wife Francis. He was born in Kildare, Ireland, on 1 November 1835 and entered the Army as an ensign in the 2nd Regiment in 1852. He was promoted lieutenant in 1854 and was sent to the Cape – the first of several significant associations with southern Africa. He served in the 8th Frontier War and remained in the area until 1860, employed as a surveyor and magistrate, during which time he was responsible for laying out several settler villages. In 1860 he served in China, and was present in the attack on the Dagu Forts and the advance on Beijing. In 1862 he passed through Staff College and between 1871 and 1873 he was professor of military administration at Sandhurst.

In 1873 he was in command of Sir Garnet Wolseley's transport department during the invasion of Asante. This placed him squarely within Wolseley's influential circle of associates, the so-called 'Asante Ring', and he emerged from the campaign with a CB and a brevet-colonelcy. In 1875 he served on Wolseley's staff during his tenure as lieutenant governor of Natal. On his return home he was appointed first military secretary and then private secretary to Lord Lytton, the governor general of India. When, in June 1879, Wolseley was dispatched to Zululand to supersede Lord Chelmsford, he asked Lytton to release Colley, and Colley duly returned to Africa as Wolseley's chief of staff. He served in that capacity throughout Wolseley's pacification operations at the close of hostilities and during the political settlement of Zululand.

When the British envoy in Kabul, Sir Louis Cavagnari, was murdered in September 1879, Lytton requested Colley's return. As a result he was not present during Wolseley's conquest of King Sekhukhune later that year, but in 1880 he succeeded to Wolseley's position as Governor of Natal, High Commissioner for Southern Africa and Commander-in-Chief of British troops. He had not long taken up this post, however, when the Boer population of the Transvaal – which Britain had annexed in 1877 – broke into revolt. A number of British garrisons across the Transvaal were besieged, forcing Colley to advance from Natal to their relief. The Boers quickly blocked his passage through the Kahlamba mountains at the Laing's Nek pass. Despite having inadequate troops at his disposal, Colley had little choice but to attempt to fight his way through. His frontal attack at Laing's Nek was defeated on 28 January 1881, and when he attempted to clear his lines of communication he was very nearly trapped at Schuinshoogte (Ingogo) on

8 February. These defeats led to an armistice, imposed from London, but on the night of 26-27 February Colley and a mixed force under his command occupied Majuba hill, which overlooked the Boer positions. Colley's intentions remain the subject of debate, but it seems that he had hoped to gain political advantage during the negotiations by holding this apparently commanding position. In fact, the Boers launched an energetic counter-attack, making good use of the sheltered approaches to the mountain, and the British position was overrun; Colley was shot through the head and killed. His body was removed to the foot of the mountain and buried in the Mount Prospect camp. Colley had been admired and respected for his personal manner, but the subtle barb implicit in Sir Evelyn Wood's comment, 'he was the best-*instructed* soldier I ever met', reflected the disparity between his intellectual skills and his achievements as a field commander.

Crealock, Henry Hope

Crealock was born in 1831, the son of William Crealock of Langerton, a village near Bideford in Devon. He was educated at Rugby School and was commissioned as an ensign into the 90th Regiment in 1848. He was promoted lieutenant in 1852 and captain in 1854. He first saw action with his regiment in the Crimean War where he took part in the siege of Sevastopol, being mentioned in dispatches for his part in the attack on The Quarries. He was promoted major and made Deputy Acting Quartermaster General at the Crimean Headquarters in September 1855 and later at the base at Constantinople.

In 1857 he was given the same position in the 1st China War and was present in the fighting around Canton. During the Indian Mutiny he served in the actions around Rohilkund. In 1861, as a lieutenant colonel, he was appointed military secretary to Lord Elgin, the British ambassador to China and, when fighting broke out again, Crealock served on the headquarters staff. He then served in Gibraltar and was employed in diplomatic posts at the Tsarist court in St Petersburg and in Vienna. In 1870 he was promoted major general. From 1874 to 1877 he was deputy quartermaster general in Ireland.

When Lord Chelmsford appealed for reinforcements in the aftermath of Isandlwana, the War Office dispatched four major generals to assist him, one of whom was Crealock. He was designated to take command of the entire campaign if Lord Chelmsford was incapacitated, and was given command of the 1st Division, which comprised Colonel Pearson's old coastal column augmented by regiments dispatched as reinforcements. The coastal districts had largely been pacified by Chelmsford's victory at kwaGingindlovu on 2 April, and Crealock's objectives were to ensure that they remained so by destroying important royal homesteads in the district. He was also to attempt to effect a landing stage on the beach where supplies might be landed by sea. Although the size of the 1st Division was indeed sufficient to intimidate Zulus living in the coastal districts, Crealock's advance was hampered by a shortage of supply wagons. So slow was his advance that his column was dubbed 'Crealock's Crawlers'. The Division built a series of supply depots along its line of advance and destroyed the emaNgweni and Hlalangubo *amakhanda*. It also established a beachhead at Port Durnford, although the strong surf and open beach meant that the landing of supplies remained problematic. Towards the end of June a number of important *amakhosi* in the coastal sector began to surrender. On 4 July, however, Lord Chelmsford defeated the main Zulu army at oNdini, and the actions of the 1st Division became largely irrelevant. Crealock returned to the UK and retired from the Army in 1884. Like his brother John – Chelmsford's assistant military secretary – Henry Crealock was a talented amateur artist. He died in 1891 at the age of sixty-one.

Crealock, John North

Crealock was born on 21 May 1836, the younger brother of Henry Hope Crealock. He was educated at Rugby School and was commissioned as an ensign into the 95th Regiment in 1854. In 1856 the 95th was ordered to the Cape garrison but had scarcely arrived when it was ordered to India on the outbreak of the Mutiny. Crealock took part in the siege and capture of Kotah and the Battle of Kotah-ki-Serai, where he was wounded.

He was promoted lieutenant in 1855, captain in 1859 and major in 1875. He spent much of the 1860s in India before being transferred to Ireland and then Aldershot where he was Deputy Assistant Adjutant-General.

In 1869 he married Marion Lloyd and the couple had three children. During his time at Aldershot he worked with Sir Frederic Thesiger, later Lord Chelmsford, and when Thesiger took up the command of troops in southern Africa he asked for Crealock as his assistant military secretary ('assistant' referring to rank; Thesiger had no other military secretary) Thesiger arrived at the Cape in February 1878 and took command at the beginning of March. Crealock was to serve with him throughout his time in Africa. He accompanied the then Lord Chelmsford during the invasion of Zululand on 11 January, and was present with him throughout the Isandlwana campaign. He seldom left Chelmsford's side and was with him during the Battles of kwaGingindlovu – where he was slightly wounded – and Ulundi.

Crealock's temperament was a major factor in the controversies surrounding the Isandlwana debacle. Since Chelmsford was a conservative officer who did not trouble to employ a trained staff, Crealock was his chief of staff by default. He was arrogant and facetious, protective of his position and jealous of Chelmsford's attention. He worked to keep other staff officers at a distance. His manner contributed to the difficult relationship between the Headquarters and Column staffs during the Isandlwana campaign and caused Colonel Glyn's staff officer, Major Clery, to describe Crealock as 'swaggering, false, self-sufficient, superficial and flippant'. Wolseley – who was, of course, a snob – commented that Crealock was not 'a gentleman, his father was not a gentleman before him and he can't help that'.

Many of Chelmsford's critics accused Crealock of interfering in Chelmsford's management of the war and certainly he does not seem to have been overly efficient, as the number of poorly worded orders to emanate from Chelmsford's staff indicates.

At the end of the war he was promoted to the position of military secretary but lost the post almost immediately on Wolseley's assumption of command.

He returned to England with Chelmsford and remained loyal to him, but for the most part Crealock's reputation had suffered during the war. He commanded the 95th Regiment from 1880 to 1885 and served in the Egyptian campaign of 1882, where he was appointed commander of Alexandria.

His later career was spent in peacetime postings between England and India. He commanded the Derbyshire and Aldershot districts before being given command of the Madras district in 1893.

He died at Rawalpindi on 26 April 1895, a major general and a CB.

For all his lack of personal skills he was a talented amateur artist and recorded many aspects of his time in both the Cape Frontier and Anglo-Zulu Wars.

Curling, Henry Thomas

Henry Thomas Curling was born at Ramsgate on 27 July 1847. He was educated at Marlborough before entering the Royal Military Academy, Woolwich, at the age of seventeen. Notwithstanding being short-sighted, he was commissioned into the Royal Artillery in 1868. He was sent to South Africa in 1878 with N Battery, 5th Brigade and served in the closing stages of the 9th Frontier War. The battery was later attached to the Centre Column for the invasion of Zululand and accompanied the advance to Isandlwana. Early on the morning of 22 January Lord Chelmsford split his command, taking a large detachment to attack a Zulu force which he believed was assembling in the Mangeni hills. He took with him four of N/5 battery's guns; Curling was left in camp in charge of the remaining two-gun section. He deployed the guns when the Zulu attack began but he was then superseded by his senior officer, Major Stewart Smith, who arrived back at that moment from Mangeni. As the firing line collapsed the guns were withdrawn but even as they reached the camp it had been overrun by the Zulus. Most of the gunners were killed during the retreat and the guns themselves were overturned as they descended into the Manzimnyama valley. Curling and Smith rode on but Smith was killed during the final descent to the Mzinyathi River. Curling wrote a dramatic description of the battle, the contents of which were largely ignored by the official enquiry on the grounds that it contained 'nothing of value'. In fact it was the only account from a surviving officer who fought in the front line at Isandlwana. He wrote:

> Just a line to say I am alive after a most wonderful escape...our camp was attacked by overwhelming numbers of Zulus. The camp was taken and out of a force of 700 white men only 30 escaped. All my men except me were killed and the guns taken...The whole column has retreated into Natal again and we are expecting hourly to be attacked. Of course everything has been lost, not a blanket left.

Curling's health suffered as a result of his experiences and some unfortunate remarks he passed in a letter home – which was later published – caused offence among colonial troops serving with the column; Curling was obliged to apologize. After the Zulu campaign he was promoted captain and sent to the war in Afghanistan. He was attached to C/3 Battery, stationed in Kabul. He returned to England after three years without leave, and was promoted major at Aldershot. In 1895, he was promoted to lieutenant colonel and made commanding officer of the Royal Artillery in Egypt. He retired as full colonel in 1902. He died a bachelor at Ramsgate on New Year's Day 1910.

Dalton, James Langley VC

Dalton was born in Holborn, London about 1834 or 1835 and was working as a stationery shop assistant when he left to join the Army on 20 November 1849. He was enrolled in the 85th Regiment – probably lying about his age – and served with it in Ireland, Mauritius and at the Cape, where he saw action in the 8th Cape Frontier War (1851-1853). He was a highly-regarded soldier who qualified for good conduct pay and rose to the rank of sergeant. He returned to England and in March 1862 transferred to the Commissariat Staff Corps as a corporal. In 1863 he was promoted colour sergeant and later master sergeant. He served in Canada between 1868 and 1871, taking part in Sir Garnet Wolseley's Red River expedition. In 1870 the Army's commissariat services were reorganized and Dalton was transferred to the Army Service Corps. He returned to England in 1871 and was discharged with the rank of staff sergeant.

During the mid-1870s he went to southern Africa and, on the outbreak of the 9th Frontier War in 1877, he volunteered to serve again with the commissariat. There was a desperate shortage of experienced commissariat staff and he was accepted with the rank of Acting Assistant Commissary (equiv-alent to a lieutenant). He was involved in organizing supplies to roving columns and scattered camps and found himself in charge of the stores at the post of Ibeka which was in the forefront of the fighting and at one point was cut off by the amaXhosa and under constant threat of attack.

At the end of the war Dalton resigned his appointment but volunteered again with the imminent outbreak of the Zulu campaign. He was posted to join the No. 3 (Centre) Column and, together with civilian storekeeper Lewis (Louis) Byrne, he rode to Helpmekaar from Pietermaritzburg in pouring rain, arriving on New Year's Day 1879. Both men were then attached to the supply depot at Rorke's Drift, commanded by Acting Commissary Walter Dunne, where stores were being accumulated to go forward to the Column. On 22 January, however, the column's camp was overrun at Isandlwana and elements of the Zulu reserve crossed the Mzinyathi River and attacked Rorke's Drift.

There can be no doubt that Dalton's role in the defence was

crucial; from the first he took a firm line that the post should be defended. His long career as an NCO, his commanding presence and his recent experience on the Cape frontier gave him an authority which Commissariat officers might otherwise have lacked in field situations. It is possible Dalton had his experiences at Ibeka in mind, and hoped that a show of resolution might be enough to deter the Zulus from attacking. That proved not to be the case, but once the battle began Dalton constantly moved around the post, encouraging the men. He was on the rear barricade, throwing his hat at the enemy in exultation when the first assault was checked; then, when the Zulu attack moved to the front, he was there, fighting with the bayonet. When a Zulu seized the muzzle of one man's rifle, and was about to spear him, Dalton shot the Zulu down. He paced about the front barricade, firing repeatedly over the ramparts at each fresh Zulu rush. Late in the evening a Zulu sprang onto the barricade near Dalton, who called out 'Pot that fellow!'. The Zulu was shot down but, a few seconds later, Dalton stiffened, shot through the shoulder. He turned and handed his rifle to Lieutenant Chard so calmly that Chard did not at first realize how seriously Dalton was hit. The injury was a bad one and Dalton was taken to Surgeon Reynolds' makeshift dressing station for attention. Nevertheless, he continued to cheer on the men throughout the night.

After the battle was over he was sent first to Helpmekaar and then to Pietermaritzburg for medical care. His role in the fight earned him the admiration of the defenders and, when B Company marched through Natal at the end of the war, they spotted Dalton in the crowd of spectators and spontaneously cheered him. His name was not, however, among those first recommended for the Victoria Cross, probably because he was a Commissariat officer; it was finally gazetted on 18 November 1879 after considerable lobbying. He was presented with the award by General Hugh Clifford VC at Fort Napier, Pietermaritzburg, on 16 January 1880.

Once his wound had healed Dalton was given the permanent rank of Sub-Assistant Commissary and served at Fort Napier until February 1880 when he returned to England on half-pay. When he left the Army he gave his place of intended residence as Port Elizabeth and by 1886 he was in the goldfields at Barberton in the Transvaal. Just before Christmas he went to stay with an old friend, a retired soldier who ran a hotel in Port Elizabeth on the Eastern Cape. He was taken ill early in the New Year, spent the day of 7 January 1887 in his bed and died suddenly during the night. He was given a quiet burial in the Roman Catholic cemetery in Port Elizabeth.

Drummond, the Hon. William Henry

Drummond was the third son of William Drummond, ninth Viscount Strathallan. He was born in August 1845, and went to southern Africa in the 1860s in search of adventure. He hunted extensively in Zululand for sport, scouring the Black Mfolozi bush, the Phongolo and Ngwavuma districts for game which, in the fashion of the age, he slaughtered by the wagonload. During that time he lived largely apart from European society, sharing his adventures with experienced African hunters and in doing so earned a good command of the Zulu language. His sporting reminiscence, *The Large Game and Natural History of South and South East Africa,* was published in 1875. By that point he had returned to live in Scotland, but he later went back to Natal, apparently as a civil servant.

At the beginning of the Anglo-Zulu War he volunteered his services as a civilian interpreter to Lord Chelmsford. With his family connections – the Drummonds were a leading family in Scotland and William's sister was a maid in waiting to Queen Victoria – he had no difficulty in securing a post on Chelmsford's personal staff. He served throughout the war, and was responsible for the official translation of many reports gleaned from Zulu deserters and captives. He was in charge of Chelmsford's Intelligence Department during the Gingindlovu and Ulundi campaigns. At the end of the Battle of Ulundi (4 July 1879), when the Zulus were in retreat, there was a rush among mounted British officers to be first into the oNdini complex itself. Drummond was one of those who took part in the chase, but his horse apparently became uncontrollable, and carried him unnoticed by the others into a group of retreating Zulus who, once they had recovered from their astonishment, killed him. His fate remained a mystery following Chelmsford's withdrawal from oNdini, but when Sir Garnet Wolseley re-occupied the area in August a search was made for Drummond's body. It was found on 17 August about three miles from the camp Wolseley had established in the ruins of oNdini itself. Captain A. F. Hart noted that:

> We heard from certain Zulus who had submitted to us, that after the action he had ridden forward among the retreating enemy, who, of course, killed him at once. They indicated about where this had happened, and after a long search his remains were found, and identified by some hair remaining, but principally by the boots with spurs. His bones alone remained besides, and they were duly interred by our chaplain.

Drury-Lowe, Drury Curzon

Drury Curzon Drury-Lowe was born in Derbyshire on 3 January 1830, the third son of William Drury-Lowe and his wife Caroline (née Curzon). He was educated privately and at Corpus Christi College, Oxford, where he obtained a BA. In 1855 he joined the 17th Lancers as an ensign and served with the regiment during the closing stages of the Crimean War. In 1857 he was promoted captain and in 1858 the 17th was sent to Bombay and took an active part in the suppression of the Indian Mutiny in central India. Drury-Lowe was promoted lieutenant colonel in 1866.

In February 1879, the 17th, then stationed at Hounslow and Hampton Court in England, received orders to embark for Natal in the aftermath of Isandlwana. Drury-Lowe assumed command after the commanding officer, Colonel Gonne, was shot in the leg during revolver practice. The regiment arrived in Durban in April and had a reassuring effect on the white

76

settlers in Natal; in fact, however, the impressive British-born horses took time to adjust to the climate and the regiment marched slowly to the border. Together with the 1st Dragoon Guards, it was formed into a cavalry brigade under Major General Sir Frederick Marshall. Lord Chelmsford was initially undecided how best to deploy it, and indeed there was talk that it might be confined to the lines of communication. In the event the Cavalry Brigade was attached to the 2nd Division.

On 21 May Marshall commanded most of the brigade, including the 17th, in a visit to the old Isandlwana battlefield, to hastily bury some of the dead and recover wagons abandoned since the disaster in January. On 1 June the 2nd Division crossed into Zululand, screened by the cavalry. That same day the Prince Imperial of France was killed in a skirmish on the Tshotshozi River; on the 2nd the 17th formed part of the guard appointed to recover his body. Drury-Lowe was among the officers who lifted the body on an improvised bier of lances to the ambulance wagon. On the 5th, Irregulars attached to the Flying Column encountered a Zulu force defending homesteads at the foot of eZungeni hill, overlooking the uPoko River. After a brief skirmish, in which they set fire to some huts, the Irregulars retired but in the meantime Marshall had brought forward the Cavalry Brigade from the 2nd Division. Drury-Lowe asked that the 17th be allowed to deploy and Marshall agreed. They crossed the uPoko but the Zulus retired on their approach and a charge through mealie-fields below the huts struck air. As the Lancers regrouped a Zulu marksman shot Lieutenant Frith, the 17th's adjutant, through the heart as he took an order beside Drury-Lowe. The 17th withdrew, and Frith was buried close to the 2nd Division camp at Fort Newdigate.

The skirmish was a telling reminder of the need to employ cavalry in the manner to which they were best suited. Nevertheless, the Lancers continued to play a prominent part in the advance on oNdini, and on 26 June they formed part of a sizeable foray into the emaKhosini valley – the ancestral Zulu heartland – which destroyed a number of venerable royal homesteads.

On 4 July they were present with the force commanded by Lord Chelmsford which crossed the White Mfolozi drift onto the Ulundi plain. In the battle which ensued, the Lancers remained inside the British square until the Zulu attacks were largely spent. Then, on Lord Chelmsford's order 'Go at them!', they emerged from the square and formed up. Here Drury-Lowe was hit by a spent bullet that knocked him from the saddle but, not seriously injured, he remounted and gave the order to charge. The 17th inflicted considerable loss on the Zulus, forcing them away from the square and preventing them reforming. Eventually, on the far side of the plain, a number of warriors rallied on rising ground and fired a volley into their pursuers, killing Captain Wyatt-Edgell. The charge then dissolved into a series of running fights. The Zulus gave way, however, and the Lancers rode in triumph around the plain, setting fire to a number of outlying royal homesteads.

The victory meant the end of the war for the Lancers, who returned to Natal; Drury-Lowe was awarded the CB for his services. He returned to England but in 1881 was sent out to Natal again, commanding the cavalry detachments which were intended to reinforce Sir George Colley's force in the Transvaal Rebellion. By the time Drury-Lowe had arrived in Durban, however, Colley himself was dead and the war was over.

In 1882, however, he accompanied Sir Garnet Wolseley's expedition to Egypt in command of the cavalry troops. Wolseley's force advanced on Cairo from the Suez Canal by means of the Sweetwater Canal; on 28 August General Graham's force, in the vanguard, was the subject of a strong Egyptian counter-attack. Graham's signals indicated that he was hard-pressed and Drury-Lowe hurried to support him. Allowing his men only a few minutes to rest their horses, he ordered a charge, despite the fact that it was already evening; the so-called 'Midnight Charge' swung the tide of battle and threw the Egyptians back in confusion. The decisive battle of the campaign took place at Tel-el-Kebir a fortnight later and was followed by a determined cavalry thrust which occupied

Cairo. Drury-Lowe was awarded the KCB for his services and emerged something of a public hero, hailed as 'the foremost cavalry leader of his day'. It was the highlight of his active career, for on his return to England he was made commander of the Cavalry Brigade at Aldershot and Inspector-General of Cavalry. In 1895 he was placed on the retired list and made a KCB; he died on 6 May 1908 in Bath. He had married in 1876 but the couple had no children.

Dunne, Walter Alphonsus

Dunne was born in Cork, Ireland, on 10 February 1853, the third son of James Dunne of Dublin. He joined the Army's Control Department (which in 1875 became the Commissariat and Transport Department) as a sub-assistant commissary (the equivalent of a second lieutenant) on 9 April 1873. After training he was stationed in Dublin until 1877; in 1875 he was promoted assistant commissary (lieutenant). In 1877 he was dispatched to southern Africa. He served throughout the 9th Cape Frontier War, first serving with a column commanded by Colonel Glyn of the 1/24th, and then attached to a detachment commanded by Colonel Wood. He was present in the fighting around the Xhosa stronghold of Ntaba-ka-Ndoda.

When the Frontier campaign ended he was sent to the Transvaal to join Colonel Rowlands' abortive campaign against the baPedi of King Sekhukhune. At the end of the year he was ordered to Helpmekaar to join the No.3 (Centre) Column assembling there – a demanding journey in which he covered 100 miles in two days. With the advance of the column into Zululand on 11 January 1879, Dunne remained at Rorke's Drift. He was the senior commissariat officer there and was responsible for supervising the stockpile of supplies which was due to go forward to the column at Isandlwana on 22 January. With the Zulu attack on Isandlwana the supplies were never sent and, indeed, formed the basis of the barricades erected to protect the mission buildings at Rorke's Drift. Dunne took an active part in building the defences and at the height of the battle was responsible for converting a large pile of mealie-bags in front of the storehouse into a redoubt.

For his gallantry Dunne was promoted deputy commissary (captain) with effect from 23 January; he was recommended for the award of the Victoria Cross but was turned down on the grounds that his actions did not warrant it – a decision influenced by the growing feeling that the garrison had received decorations enough. Dunne was appointed Commissary of Supplies with the Flying Column, took part in the second invasion of Zululand, and was present at the Battle of Ulundi on 4 July.

At the end of the Anglo-Zulu War he accompanied the troops under Sir Garnet Wolseley's command who were sent to attack Sekhukhune, and Dunne was present at the storming of the baPedi capital in November 1879. He remained in the Transvaal and was still there at the end of 1880 when the Boers rose in revolt against the British occupation. Dunne was sent to join the British garrison at Potchefstroom which was promptly besieged by the Boers. Some 200 British troops and 48 civilians were trapped within a small improvised fort from December 1880 to March 1881. Dunne, a staunch Catholic, read the Catholic service from the parapet every Sunday for the benefit of those who shared his faith. The garrison was finally forced to surrender but marched out of Potchefstroom with full military honours.

Dunne's health was impaired and he spent time in Natal recuperating, and here he met Winifred Bird, whom he was to marry in 1885. Dunne returned to England in April 1882, but later that year took part in the Egyptian campaign, and was present at the Battle of Tel-el-Kebir. In 1885 he fought in the operations against the Mahdists around the Red Sea port of Suakin. He returned to England for a series of staff posts, served in Mauritius from 1887 to 1889, and transferred as a lieutenant colonel to the newly formed Army Service Corps in 1888. In 1896 he was awarded the CB and in 1897 promoted colonel. He served as Assistant Director of Supplies in Gibraltar and retired in 1908. He died just five months later, on 2 July 1908, at the English Nursing Convent in Rome.

Durnford, Anthony William

Durnford was the eldest son of Edward Durnford, then a lowly lieutenant but destined to rise to become a general and Colonel Commandant of the Royal Engineers, and his wife Elizabeth. Anthony was born on 24 May 1830 at Manor Hamilton in the county of Leitrim, Ireland. He was educated in Düsseldorf, Germany, and entered the Royal Military Academy at Woolwich in July 1846. His choice of career was probably never in doubt; a member of the Durnford family had served in the Corps of Royal Engineers since 1759, and both Durnford's younger brothers, Edward and Arthur, joined the Corps. Durnford obtained a commission in the Engineers as a second lieutenant in 1848. He served in Chatham and Scotland before being posted to Ceylon in 1851. On 15 September 1854 he married Frances Tranchell; the marriage was not destined to be a happy one. Although they had a daughter, Frances, to whom Durnford was devoted, they lost several children in infancy and the marriage soured. Durnford took solace in gambling and the couple later separated but never divorced. Durnford remained in Ceylon until 1856 when he was posted to Malta. In 1858 he returned to England. He was in Gibraltar between 1860 and 1864 when he was sent to China. He collapsed with heat apoplexy on the journey, landed in Ceylon and returned to England. In 1871 he accepted a post at the Cape.

Durnford's early experiences in southern Africa defined his career. Although he seems to have put his marriage problems behind him and contained his gambling he was clearly ill at ease in himself and he repressed his anxieties in energetic physical exercise. He was employed briefly on the Cape frontier but was then sent to Natal. He arrived in time to join Theophilus Shepstone's expedition to 'crown' King Cetshwayo in August 1873. Durnford returned hugely impressed by what he had seen and by the Zulu people. About this time he established a friendly relationship with Bishop Colenso; like Colenso he admired and respected the Zulu people although he was too much a believer in military duty to question British policies in the region.

Shortly after his return, Durnford was appointed chief of staff to Lieutenant Colonel Milles, the officer commanding British troops in Natal, who was about to embark on military action against the 'rebellious' *inkosi* Langalibalele kaMthimkhulu of the amaHlubi people. Langalibalele's followers had fallen foul of the colonial authorities because their migrant labourers had received guns in lieu of payment from Kimberley diamond diggers. Langalibalele had been ordered to surrender the arms, had procrastinated, and, on seeing colonial troops mustering for Cetshwayo's coronation expedition, had assumed he was about to be attacked and had fled to the Kahlamba mountain passes in the hope of escaping to BaSotholand. Durnford was given command of a detachment of colonial troops and ordered, quite literally, to cut Langalibalele off at the pass. Durnford's party set out on the evening of 2 November 1873 for the mountain foothills. Their understanding of the topography was hazy and they got lost; ascending a particularly steep and grassy slope Durnford's horse, Chieftain, lost its footing and he fell, his body rolling over for fifty yards down the slope. When his men rushed to assist him they found Durnford had dislocated his left shoulder and badly cut his head. He insisted in continuing, and the party eventually reached the summit of the mountains. Here they rode on until they encountered amaHlubi working their way up from below. The main escape route appeared to be by way of the Bushman's Pass and hundreds of amaHlubi, mostly men under arms, were already moving through it. Durnford deployed his men across the pass and attempted to prevent the crowd moving past. The mood among the amaHlubi became belligerent but Durnford had been ordered not to fire the first shot if possible. One of the amaHlubi fired a shot and a sudden scrimmage broke out; Durnford's interpreter, Elijah Nkambule, was killed at his side and Durnford himself was stabbed through the elbow of his already-injured left arm. Three of the colonial troopers were killed and the survivors retreated in disarray; Langalibalele and the majority of the amaHlubi escaped into BaSotholand.

The incident left deep physical and psychological scars on Durnford. His left arm did not heal and was useless thereafter; he wore it thrust, Napoleon-like, into the front of his tunic. Colonial society held him to blame for the deaths of the troopers through his reluctance to open fire; he was mocked as 'Don't Fire Durnford'. His was a familiar figure, with his injured arm and long side-whiskers, and a lonely one, for he became so unpopular in Pietermaritzburg that his dog was poisoned and he was forced to live in the barracks at Fort Napier. It was during this period that he came to rely on his friendship with Bishop Colenso – who was already isolated from colonial society because he championed unpopular African causes – and formed a relationship with Colenso's daughter, Frances. Although this relationship has been the subject of much speculation ever since, it is unlikely it ever developed into a full love affair; Francis was several years younger than Durnford and both were bound by contemporary propriety. Durnford was, moreover, still married and, in the aftermath of the Bushman's Pass affair he clung more tightly than ever to his sense of honour.

Despite growing misgivings about the conduct of the campaign, Durnford served in the punitive actions against the amaHlubi and their neighbours, the amaPhutile, which followed Langalibalele's 'rebellion'. Langalibalele was later surrendered to the colonial authorities, tried, and exiled to the Cape.

In 1876 Durnford returned to England but he was back in Natal a year later. In 1878, as the colony's senior Engineer, he served on the Boundary Commission set up by Sir Henry Bulwer to investigate the disputed border between the Transvaal and Zulu kingdom; the commission found largely in favour of the Zulu claims. With the political crisis accelerating, Durnford was asked by Lieutenant General Thesiger (Lord Chelmsford) to plan the formation of an African auxiliary force to support the British invasion. Although some elements of Durnford's outline were abandoned for reasons of expense, the blueprint was largely responsible for the creation of the Natal Native Contingent in November 1878. Durnford himself was given command of No. 2 Column, which was composed almost entirely of auxiliary troops. He took unusual pains to secure good calibre officers who trained his men as efficiently as possible.

Durnford's column was placed on the high escarpment above the Middle Drift over the Thukela River. It was given a supportive role, to guard against Zulu attacks on that stretch of the border, or to advance in concert with the main invading columns as needed. On 14 January, three days after the war began, Durnford, acting on local information, decided to take his column down to the Middle Drift, an action that provoked a sharp rebuke from Chelmsford. Probably as a result of this, on the 16th, Chelmsford ordered Durnford to move to a point upstream of the Middle Drift, and closer to the Centre Column. On the 20th, when Chelmsford moved the Centre Column forward to Isandlwana, Durnford was ordered to Rorke's Drift. When, early on the morning of the 22nd, Chelmsford decided to advance again with part of his force to reinforce his detachments at Mangeni, he ordered – almost as an afterthought – Durnford forward to Isandlwana.

Durnford arrived at the camp at Isandlwana at about 10.30 a.m. on the 22nd. He had presumably expected to find further orders from Lord Chelmsford clarifying his intentions, but there were none. The commander at the camp, Lieutenant Colonel Pulleine, reported to Durnford that after Chelmsford's departure Zulus had been seen in some strength on the iNyoni ridge immediately above the camp. As a brevet colonel, Durnford was senior to Pulleine but he saw nothing in Chelmsford's orders to suggest that he was expected to take command of the camp. Instead, he decided to take his command out from Isandlwana, to split it in two and scour the iNyoni heights. His fear was not for the safety of the camp, but that the unknown Zulu force might be attempting to cut Lord Chelmsford off from his supports.

1. William Allan.

2. Percy Barrow c. 1881.
(SB. Bourquin Collection).

3. Lord William Beresford, c.1869.
(9/12th Lancers Museum)

4. Prince Louis Napoleon Bonaparte; one of a number of portraits taken in Durban on his departure for the front.

5. Anthony Clarke Booth.
(Ron Sheeley Collection).

6. Frank Bourne, c.1915.   *(RRW Museum)*

7. Gonville Bromhead.
(Ron Sheeley Collection).

8. Edward Browne, c.1900.
(Ron Sheeley Collection)

9. Redvers Buller in determined pose, late 1879. *(Ron Sheeley Collection)*

10. Brenton Carey, photographed on his return from Zululand. *(Private collection)*

11. Ronald Campbell, c.1874. *(Ron Sheeley Collection)*

12. John Chard.

13. Lord Chelmsford, photographed at the end of the Anglo-Zulu War.
(Ron Sheeley Collection)

14. Cornelius Clery, c.1869.
(MOD/Rai Engand)

15. William Cochrane in the 1890s.

16. Nevill Coghill, photographed shortly before the invasion of Zululand.
(Ron Sheeley Collection)

7. Sir George Pomeroy Colley, c.1874.
(Ron Sheeley Collection)

18. Henry Hope Crealock, c. 1869.
(Ron Sheeley Collection)

9. John North Crealock, c.1879.

20. Henry Curling, c.1900.

21. James Langley Dalton.

22. Walter Dunne.

23. Drury Curzon Drury-Lowe.

24. Anthony Durnford.

25. Edward Essex, c.1877.
(MOD/Rai England)

26 Archibald Forbes in the 1880s.
(Ron Sheeley Collection)

28. Sir Henry Bartle Frere.
(Ron Sheeley Collection)

27. Edmund Fowler.

29. Alan Gardner.
(F.W.D. Jackson Collection)

30. Richard Glyn c.1872.
(Ron Sheeley Collection)

31. Robert Hackett.
(Royal Archives, Windsor Castle)

32. Henry Harford, probably photographed at the end of the Zulu campaign.
(Local History Museums, Durban)

33. Arthur Harness.
(Royal Archives, Windsor Castle)

34. Richard Harrison, 1874.
(MOD/Rai England)

35. Arthur Fitzroy Hart, c.1899.
(Ron Sheeley Collection)

36. Henry Harward.

37. Fred Hitch.

38. Alfred Henry Hook.

39. Robert Jones.

40. William Jones.

41. William Knox Leet, 1880.
    (Royal Archives, Windsor Castle)

42. Henry Lysons.

43. Sir Frederick Marshall, sketched on
    campaign in Zululand 1879.
    (National Army Museum)

44. Richard Marter.
    (Royal Archives, Windsor Castle)

45. Teignmouth Melvill.
(Ron Sheeley Collection)

46. Archibald Berkley Milne, 1879.
(Royal Archives Windsor Castle)

47. Edward Newdigate.

48. Charles Pearson, on his return from
Zululand.   *(Ron Sheeley Collection)*

49. Melton Prior, 'The Screaming Billiard-Ball'.

50. Henry Pulleine.

51. James Henry Reynolds, c.1890.

52. Hugh Rowlands, c.1890.

53. Francis Broadfoot Russell.

54. John Cecil Russell.
(9/12th Lancers' Museum)

55. George Smith, c.1885.

56. Horace Smith-Dorrien, c.1879.

57. Sir Herbert Stewart, c. 1882.
(Ron Sheeley Collection)

58. William Penn Symons, c. 1876.
(Ron Sheeley Collection)

59. Samuel Wassall.

60. John Williams. (*Fielding*)

61. Sir Garnet Wolseley, c.1877.

62. Sir Henry Evelyn Wood, c.1881.
(Ron Sheeley Collection)

63. Richard Warren Wynne

64. Staff of the Flying Column photographed in Zululand, Evelyn Wood centre. Sitting right is Cornelius Clery; sitting on the ground Henry Lysons. Standing second from the left is Lord William Beresford, and second from the right Edward Woodgate.

(SB Bourquin Collection)

Durnford left the camp about 11.30 a.m. At that point his baggage train, with his ammunition, had not yet arrived in camp, and he left without knowing where it would park. While he sent detachments onto the heights he took his own (mounted) command at a canter along the foot of the escarpment, passing the iThusi knoll and progressing a further two miles. Here he was warned by vedettes on the heights that a Zulu army was nearby; he reacted incredulously to the news but minutes later the Zulus came into view. He was facing the left 'horn' of the Zulu army. He deployed his men in line and conducted a disciplined retreat towards the camp, halting regularly to fire at the pursuing Zulus. Rounding iThusi he found the survivors of the rocket battery – part of his command which had trailed in his wake and which had been overrun by Zulu skirmishers. He retreated until he reached the Nyogane donga, nearly a mile from the camp. Here he made a stand, dismounting his men and deploying them under the cover of the donga's banks. They opened such a heavy fire on the left 'horn' that it was checked. Durnford himself paced about behind his men, encouraging them and clearing their jammed carbines with his one good arm, all the frustrations of his past career expiated in a moment of intense action. In fact, however, his position was a dangerous one. It was too far out from the camp to be supported properly by Pulleine's infantry, and when his men began to grow short of ammunition Durnford's riders could not find their reserve supplies in the confusion of the camp. He was, moreover, being outflanked on both sides; elements from the Zulu centre were beginning to press between him and Pulleine's nearest company, while the left 'horn', extending even further to its left, began to cross the donga downstream.

Durnford had little option but to abandon his position and fall back on the camp. In doing so he left Pulleine's right flank exposed and precipitated the collapse of the British line. The fragmentary evidence that survives suggests that Durnford rode into camp to seek out Pulleine and that shortly afterwards the infantry were ordered to withdraw from their advanced positions. The Zulus exploited this move with a fierce charge, and the line broke. Durnford excused most of his own men from the field then returned to join a group of colonial troops who were attempting to block the road through the camp against the attack of the Zulu left. Durnford took command of this group until they were overrun and all killed.

Durnford's actions at Isandlwana have remained controversial. In the recriminations which followed, Lord Chelmsford's staff openly blamed him for the disaster, stressing that he had failed to take responsibility for the camp as a whole and that his movements had prevented the employment of a more realistic defensive procedure. There is some justification to both criticisms although when Durnford's body was found on the battlefield on 21 May 1879 the orders found on it from Lord Chelmsford included no explicit instruction to take command of the camp. Durnford's death undoubtedly made him a scapegoat for the wider failings of the campaign.

In October 1879 Durnford's body was exhumed at Bishop Colenso's instigation and removed to Pietermaritzburg where it was re-interned in the military cemetery at Fort Napier. Durnford's brother Edward and Frances Colenso, defended Durnford's reputation for the rest of their lives.

Essex, Edward

Essex was born on 13 November 1847 in Camden Town, London, the fourth child of Thomas Essex, who owned a tannery business, and his wife Margaret. Perhaps prompted by a realization that the tannery business would pass to their father's eldest son, both Edward Essex and his elder brother Thomas opted for a military career. Edward passed the entrance exam and entered Sandhurst in February 1866. He passed out third in his class, a position which entitled him to seek a rank as ensign without purchase. In March 1867 he was appointed to the 75th Regiment. His early career was spent in peacetime postings in Gibraltar and Hong Kong, where he was appointed adjutant. In May 1871 he purchased a captain's commission within his regiment – one of the last officers in the

British Army to do so, as the purchase system was abolished shortly afterwards. In October 1871 the 75th were transferred to southern Africa for garrison duty in Natal and on the Eastern Cape. Although Essex took a significant period of leave during this period, the posting gave him experience of local conditions which presumably influenced his decision to volunteer as a 'special service' officer on the eve of the Anglo-Zulu War.

At the end of 1874 the 75th returned to the UK and barracks in Ireland and, at the beginning of 1876, Essex embarked upon a two-year course at the Staff College. Upon its completion he was appointed Instructor of Musketry to the Manchester garrison, but with Lord Chelmsford's appeal for officers to volunteer for special duties in the prelude to the Zulu campaign Essex volunteered. On 31 October 1878 he sailed for Natal. On his arrival he was appointed Director of Transport to No. 3 Column, an unglamorous but essential job which consisted of assembling sufficient horses, oxen and wagons to facilitate transport of the column's baggage train. As an assistant he was given the young Lieutenant Horace Smith-Dorrien of the 95th Regiment.

The outbreak of war on 11 January ushered in testing times for Essex and the column's tiny Transport Staff, for the wagons had to be ferried across the Mzinyathi River at Rorke's Drift and stores stockpiled for the advance. On the 20th the column moved forward to Isandlwana. Once the supply wagons were unloaded they were due to return to Rorke's Drift to pick up fresh supplies, but with the discovery of Zulu forces in the Mangeni area on the evening of the 21st – and Chelmsford's decision to advance with part of his command to meet them – this plan was abandoned. Captain Edward Essex found himself without any particular duties to perform on the 22nd. He was writing letters in his tent when the sound of distant gunfire heralded the discovery of the Zulu army:

About noon a sergeant came into my tent and told me that firing was to be heard behind the hill where the company of the 1st Battalion 24th had been sent. I had my glasses over my shoulder and thought I might as well take my revolver, but did not trouble to put on my sword, as I thought nothing of the matter and expected to be back in half an hour to complete my letters. I got on my horse and galloped up the hill, passing a company of the 24th on its way to the front and took a message from the officer for the others on the hill.

Essex joined the 24th companies deployed on the ridges over-looking the camp and – as a former Musketry Instructor – helped direct their fire. After an extended period of firing, like the prudent officer he was, he returned to the camp to ensure a supply of reserve ammunition was brought forward before the men became short. He found that his junior, Smith-Dorrien, had already been rebuffed by the quartermaster of the nearest supply, Bloomfeld of the 2nd/24th. Bloomfield was concerned that Chelmsford had ordered that the 2nd Battalion reserve be kept ready for dispatch to Mangeni should it be needed. In one of the most important comments on the man-agement of the infantry companies to emerge from Isandlwana, Essex confirmed that he overruled Bloomfield's objections and sent a considerable quantity of ammunition to the firing lines:

> The two companies which had been moved from the hill were now getting short of ammunition, so I went to the camp to bring up a fresh supply. I got such men as were not engaged, bandsmen, cooks, etc., to assist me, and sent them up to the line under charge of an officer, and I followed with more ammunition in a mule cart. In loading the later I helped the Quartermaster of the 2nd Battalion 24th to place the boxes in the cart, and while doing so the poor fellow was shot dead.

Despite the efforts of the 24th companies, however, the line was over-extended and when Colonel Durnford's command was forced to withdraw on the right, it collapsed. Essex rode to Durnford and found that he had:

> ...already observed the state of affairs, and was looking very serious. He asked me if I could bring some men to keep the enemy in check in our rear, but he had hardly said this when those natives who had not already stolen off turned round and rushed past us followed by thousands of Zulus.

Essex himself joined the general rout towards the border, and after a typically fraught escape crossed the river at the flooded Sothondose's Drift. He attempted to rally the survivors on the Natal bank, but most were too exhausted and traumatized to obey him. Instead they rode together to Helpmekaar, where Essex attempted to place the post on a defensive footing in expectation of a Zulu attack. His order that the horses at the camp be turned loose, to prevent the risk of desertion was, however, widely resented by the Volunteer troops present.

No Zulu attack materialized and in the weeks that followed the arrival of British reinforcements at Durban allowed Lord Chelmsford gradually to reclaim the initiative. With the assembly of a new column – the 2nd Division – on the Zulu border in May 1879, Edward Essex was once again appointed Director of Transport. He accompanied the column in its advance to the White Mfolozi River. Although no supply wagons were taken beyond the banks of the river, Essex was determined to accompany Lord Chelmsford's attack on the royal homestead at oNdini on 4 July 1879, and was one of the few Isandlwana survivors present within the square during the Battle of Ulundi. A few days later a number of captured British weapons were recovered from the Zulus, among them the sword Essex had decided not to wear on the morning of Isandlwana.

Essex left Natal with the rank of brevet major in early 1880. With the outbreak of the Transvaal Rebellion later that year, however, he returned in December as Deputy Assistant Adjutant and Quartermaster General to the Natal Field Force then assembling under Sir George Colley. British garrisons in the Transvaal were under threat from the Boers, and Colley intended to march to their aid by forcing the Laing's Nek pass through the Kahlamba Mountains. Two initial attempts – at Laing's Nek on 28 January 1881 and Ingogo (Schuishoogte) on 8 February – were repulsed. Essex was present at both actions but survived without injury, confirming the nickname 'Lucky' he had earned at Isandlwana. On 27 February the Natal campaign ground to an ignominious halt with the death of Colley during the disastrous assault on Majuba Mountain.

Essex returned to England after the campaign. Between 1883 and 1885 he was Instructor of Musketry and Topography at Sandhurst. In May 1886 he rejoined his regiment with the rank of brevet lieutenant colonel. He was placed on the half-pay list in 1891, and retired in June 1892 with the rank of colonel commanding the 2nd Battalion Gordon Highlanders. He was to enjoy a long retirement – 'lucky' to the end – and died on 10 September 1939 in Bournemouth at the age of ninety-one.

Fielding, John VC

Fielding was born on 24 May 1857 in Abergavenny, Monmouthshire. His father, Michael, was an Irish labourer who had emigrated from Ireland in search of work; his mother Margaret was an Abergavenny girl. John was their second son; the family moved to the village of Llantarnam in 1863.

John Fielding enlisted in the Army in May 1877 under the name of John Williams. It is not clear why he enlisted under an assumed name although it was a common practice; he may have done so to avoid the disapproval of his father since military service was held in low regard in the 1870s, or to escape a family scandal. He was posted to the 2nd Battalion 24th Regiment and enrolled in B Company. He was present with the battalion when it was sent to the Cape in February 1878 to take part in the closing stages of the 9th Cape Frontier War. B Company was present in the skirmishes around Intaba-ka-Ndoda and in the Perie Bush.

At the end of 1878 the battalion was ordered to Natal to join the No.3 (Centre) Column for the invasion of Zululand. When the Column crossed the Mzinyathi River into Zululand on 11 January 1879 B Company was left to guard the Drift and supply depot which had been established at the mission station at Rorke's Drift. Shortly after noon on the 22nd the camp of the Centre Column at Isandlwana was attacked and overrun by the Zulus; at about 4.30 p.m. the post at Rorke's Drift came under attack from elements of the Zulu reserve, who had crossed the Mzinyathi River.

Private John Williams was one of six able-bodied soldiers deployed in the hospital building to assist in the defence. They defended the building room by room and, once the Zulus had set fire to the thatched roof, evacuated the patients by knocking holes in the interior walls. Williams was nominated for the Victoria Cross by Lieutenant Bromhead and the award was gazetted on 2 May 1879. B Company remained in the vicinity of Rorke's Drift until the end of the war and was then posted to Gibraltar where Williams received his award on 1 March 1880.

Williams continued to serve with the battalion in India but returned to the UK on the expiry of his period of six years' active service in 1883. He settled in Llantarnum, resumed his real name of Fielding, took work as a labourer and served with the 3rd (Militia) Battalion, South Wales Borderers, until 1904. On 15 April 1884 he married Elizabeth Murphy; Elizabeth had one daughter to a previous relationship and the couple were to have five more children. In 1914 Fielding joined the South Wales Borderers – the old 24th – as a recruiting sergeant. Sadly his son Tom, serving with the BEF, was killed during the retreat from Mons in September. Fielding retired from military life in 1922; a modest, quiet man he continued to enjoy the support of his local community and attended a number of military functions. He died on 25 November 1932 – the longest surviving Rorke's Drift VC winner – and was buried in Llantarnum with full military honours.

Forbes, Archibald

Forbes was born on 17 April 1838, the son of a Presbyterian minister in Morayshire, Scotland. He was educated at the University of Aberdeen but dropped out and lived on his inheritance until the money ran out. He then enlisted as a trooper in the Royal Dragoons. Because of his education he rose to the rank of acting quartermaster sergeant. Although he enjoyed aspects of military life, and perfected his skills as a horseman, he was bored by the routine of barrack-room life and amused himself by writing articles on military history and anecdotes of service life, several of which were published under a pseudonym.

In 1867, he purchased his discharge from the Army with the intention of making his living as a journalist. After a difficult start, he was offered a job by the *Morning Advertiser* on a 'pay when used' basis to cover the Franco-Prussian War which had just broken out in France. He jumped at the chance and his early reports earned him a better offer from *The London Daily News*. Forbes attached himself to the Prussian army, largely because the Prussians had recognized the importance of the press and allowed journalists access to command decisions even at senior levels. Forbes came under fire at the early Battle of Saarbrucken – a battle which, ironically, was the baptism of fire for the young French Prince Imperial, whom Forbes would later meet in Zululand – and accompanied the successful Prussian advance towards Paris itself. Here Forbes, moving between the lines, had a narrow escape when he was seized by a French mob who mistook him for a spy and expressed their intention to drown him in a fountain. He was rescued in the nick of time by members of the French National Guard, taken before a magistrate and later released after the magistrate's sister recognized his name. He returned to London to dash out a quick book on his exploits before visiting Paris again to report on the last dreadful days of the Commune.

Forbes' vigorous dispatches from France, honed by his intimate knowledge of military affairs, had established his reputation as a leading war correspondent. In 1874 he covered the Carlist War in Spain and in 1876 he travelled to the Balkans where the Serbs, encouraged by the Russians, had risen in revolt against rule by Ottoman Turkey. The revolt was characterized by extraordinary brutality on both sides and Forbes himself was once captured by a Turkish patrol. He was only saved from torture when his quick-thinking Serbian servant produced a fez and, addressing the soldiers in perfect Turkish, claimed that Forbes had been granted a free passage by the Turkish high command. Forbes escaped, but in the end the Serbs were defeated. The conflagration spread, however, drawing Russia into a war against the Turks which was largely fought out in Bulgaria. Forbes again covered this conflict, then returned via St Petersburg to London. Here he was promptly dispatched on his next assignment, to cover the war which had recently broken out in Afghanistan. The Emir of Afghanistan had recently accepted a Russian envoy in the court in Kabul, fuelling British fears of Russian influence extending to the borders of India. British troops invaded with the intention of establishing a pro-British regime. Forbes arrived in time to witness the storming of the fort at Ali Musjid, and was caught up in skirmishing in the Khyber Pass, in the course of which he saved a soldier's life by pressing his thumbs into a bullet wound in the man's leg, and thereby checking the bleeding.

With a British Resident successfully installed in Kabul, Forbes thought the war over and travelled to Burma to interview the Burmese king, Thibaw. He was in Burma when the *Daily News* ordered his urgent recall; the news of Isandlwana had reached London, and Forbes was sent to the Cape. He arrived in April, as Lord Chelmsford was preparing to mount the second invasion of Zululand. With his cavalry contacts, Forbes largely attached himself to the Cavalry Brigade. He met the Prince Imperial, and exchanged stories of their adventures in the Franco-Prussian War. On 21 May a strong detachment from the Cavalry Brigade visited the Isandlwana battlefield in order to recover serviceable wagons. Forbes wrote a vivid account of the desolate battlefield which has since become a classic. On the evening of 1 June Forbes was dining with officers of the Cavalry Brigade when Colonel Richard Harrison entered with the news that the Prince Imperial had been killed in a skirmish. Forbes hurriedly sought out and interviewed four of the troopers who had survived the incident, and the following morning accompanied the Cavalry Brigade in the search for the bodies. He was apparently the first journalist to discover the Prince's body. Forbes was not afraid to voice his opinions and was openly critical of Lieutenant Carey, the officer who had survived the incident.

The presence of Forbes, Melton Prior and other journalists with the British force ensured that the story of the Prince's death attracted more column inches in the British press than had the disaster at Isandlwana. The British advance continued with some caution and Forbes, increasingly frustrated, became critical of Lord Chelmsford's leadership. Forbes was present when Chelmsford's troops finally manoeuvred into formation close to King Cetshwayo's royal homestead at oNdini on 4 July. Forbes was convinced the Zulus had missed their opportunity to attack as the troops were forming up and offered a bet that there would be no fighting; several officers wisely took him up on it, and he lost. In the ensuing battle he hurried about the square taking notes, not even distracted by a hit from a spent bullet.

After the battle was over, Forbes approached Lord Chelmsford and asked if his dispatches describing the fight could be sent that night with the official courier. Chelmsford replied that he did not intend to send a courier until the following morning, as it was growing late and the countryside was alive with bands of defeated warriors. Forbes indignantly replied 'Then, sir, I will start myself at once!' – and regretted it almost as soon as he had spoken. Nevertheless, he was committed and Colonel Wood's orderly, Lieutenant Lysons, cheerily bet Forbes £5 he would not reach the border alive – and insisted on paying him before he left, as he did not expect to see him again! Forbes set off in the gathering gloom, and by the time he had climbed the escarpment from the White

Mfolozi valley the night was pitch-black. The royal home-steads on the oNdini plain could be seen burning in the distance, and Forbes heard Zulu voices shouting to one another in the bush. Nevertheless, he reached the first of the chain of forts Chelmsford had established on the lines of communication safely and here he changed horses. He finally arrived at Landman's Drift, on the border, at 3 p.m. the following afternoon, having ridden 110 miles in twenty hours and changed his horse six times. His dispatches scooped his rivals and, not averse to publicizing his own adventures, Forbes' account of his ride was dubbed in England 'the Ride of Death'.

With the end of the war, Forbes returned to England and later applied for the official campaign medal on the grounds that he had also carried dispatches for Chelmsford's staff. Lord Chelmsford himself blocked the award, pointing out that any military messages carried by Forbes were purely private communications by his staff. This provoked Forbes to write a further attack on Lord Chelmsford's leadership throughout the war and, indeed, he became one of Chelmsford's most persistent critics.

Forbes was only in his forties but already his health was suffering as a result of his experiences. He made no attempt to cover any further campaigns, but instead contented himself with public lecture tours, in which he described his adventures, and in writing a series of reminiscences. By the time of his death in London, on 30 March 1900, he was popularly regarded as the greatest war correspondent since William Russell a generation before. He was buried in Allenvale cemetery, Aberdeen.

Fowler, Edmund John VC

Fowler was born in Waterford, Ireland, in 1861, the son of John and Bridget Fowler. He worked as a servant before enlisting in the 90th Regiment in March 1877. The battalion was posted to the Cape shortly after and Fowler was attached to the Mounted Infantry (an improvised mounted unit consisting of volunteers from infantry battalions who could ride). Fowler was one of eight men of the 90th from the MI who were selected as Colonel Wood's escort. On 28 March 1879 the escort accompanied Wood during the expedition to attack the Hlobane mountain. Wood, arriving on the field after the first assaults, came across a party of Irregulars from the Border Horse skirmishing with Zulus ensconced among boulders at the foot of the cliffs which surround the summit of Hlobane. Wood ordered his staff and escort forward to clear the Zulus; his staff officer, Captain Campbell, was killed by a shot fired at close range as he scrambled among the boulders. Wood's ADC, Second Lieutenant Lysons, and Fowler stepped over Campbell's body and fired into the rocks driving the Zulus out; Lysons then guarded the position while Fowler and other members of the escort carried Campbell's body further down the slope to be buried. On the following day, during the Battle of Khambula, Fowler remained close to Wood who was directing the battle from an exposed position outside the defences. Fowler served throughout the war and was present at the Battle of Ulundi on 4 July. In 1882 he was awarded the Victoria Cross for his part in the Hlobane battle.

Fowler purchased his discharge in January 1880 and married Mary McGuire but in 1882 he enlisted again in the Royal Irish Regiment. He took part in the Gordon Relief Expedition and rose to the rank of colour sergeant; in 1887, however, he was court-martialled, reduced to the ranks and ordered to forfeit his VC. The decision to deprive him of his award was later rescinded.

Fowler was discharged from the Army in 1900 and settled in Colchester, Essex. He later auctioned his VC, retaining minia-tures to wear. In civilian life he first ran a fruiterer's shop but when this was damaged by fire in 1910 he became a pub landlord. On one occasion he was charged with selling beer to a soldier after hours but he appeared in court wearing his VC and was acquitted. He died in Colchester on 26 March 1926, leaving a widow and five children.

Frere, Sir Bartle

Henry Bartle Edward Frere was born at Clydarck, Brecknockshire, Wales on 29 March 1815, one of a family of fourteen. He was educated in Bath and in 1834 went out to work for the East India Company in the Bombay presidency. In 1842 he was appointed private secretary to the Governor of Bombay and, after a spell of leave in England and Italy; he was appointed Resident at Sattara (1847-49), a Native state south of Bombay. On the death of the Rajah in 1848 Frere administered the state before the British formally annexed it. In 1850, at the age of thirty-five, he was promoted to be Chief Commissioner for the newly pacified province of Sind, with responsibility for the strategically important Bolan Pass, a post he held for the next nine years.

In 1856 he took sick leave and sailed for England, before returning to India in March 1857 in time to play an active part in the suppression of the Indian Mutiny. He organized for detachments to be sent to the Punjab and these were instrumental in securing the province for the Company. He served on the Governor General's Council (1859-62) and as the Governor of Bombay (1862-67). He implemented a policy of civil improvements although the collapse of the Bombay Bank, which he did little to prevent, earned his administration some criticism.

In 1867 he returned to England to serve on the Indian Council. He was widely recognized as a leading figure in British India – 'the most outstanding figure of the ten years after the mutiny' – a keen geographer (President of the Royal Geographical Society, 1873) and sanitary reformer in active partnership with Florence Nightingale. He was also an active campaigner against slavery. This prompted Lord Granville to send him out to Zanzibar in 1873 to negotiate an anti-slavery treaty and his success there raised him to the rank of Privy Councillor. The royal connection resulted in his being chosen to shepherd the Prince of Wales on the Indian Tour of 1876.

In 1877, towards the end of a highly successful career, Lord

Carnarvon offered him the post of Governor of southern Africa with a view to implementing the Confederation policy. His stature would give the project an added impetus and it seems that Frere accepted to end his career on one last success – although family sources suggest that he was also prompted by financial considerations, as he was by no means wealthy.

Frere arrived at the Cape in April 1877. It is probably fair to say that he was not a belligerent man by nature but rather a conscientious servant of Empire. He brought to southern Africa a global perspective – an awareness of the Cape's vulnerability to attacks by foreign navies – which undoubtedly spurred his determination to resolve the area's complex conflicts as quickly as possible. There was considerable opposition within the Cape Colony to Frere's ministry and the Eastern Frontier was troubled by fresh conflict with the amaXhosa. These problems had to be tackled piecemeal but underlying them Frere saw the hint of an African conspiracy to resist the consolidation of European power that he would need to scotch in order to bring the disparate white groups under British control. Under advice from men like Theophilus Shepstone – who had their own Imperial vision of the region which saw independent African states as anachronistic and a physical block on the road to expanded British interests – Frere quickly identified the existence of the Zulu kingdom as a challenge to Confederation. He determined to break up the kingdom and in doing so prove Britain's willingness to see through the Confederation policy, to discourage wider African resistance and to reassure the potentially hostile Transvaal Boers of the advantages of British rule. Although an aggressive policy towards the Zulus was not fully supported by the Colonial Office, Frere expected the campaign to be a quick one. He began a propaganda campaign, based on colonial and missionary reports which portrayed King Cetshwayo's administration as brutal and threatening to its neighbours, which was designed to prepare London for the possibility of war. He hoped to exploit the delay in communications to allow British troops to intervene in Zululand before London had time to object. The disputed boundary between the Transvaal and the Zulu kingdom offered a potential cause for military action but a Boundary Commission established by Sir Henry Bulwer, the Lieutenant Governor of Natal, declared largely in favour of the Zulu claims. While Frere contemplated his next move, the sons of the Zulu border *inkosi* Sihayo played into his hands; in the middle of 1878 they dragged back across the border two of their father's runaway wives and put them to death.

In December 1878 Frere summoned Zulu representatives to a meeting at the Lower Thukela Drift to hear the findings of the Boundary Commission; tagged onto the findings were a series of demands which amounted to little more than an ultimatum. King Cetshwayo was given thirty days to surrender Sihayo's sons, disband the Zulu army and accept a British resident at oNdini. These were demands no independent ruler could in conscience accept – as Frere intended.

Frere's plan might have been successful had not the war begun with a military disaster. Isandlwana not only destroyed Lord Chelmsford's invasion plan but also highlighted his policies in the region. Although the British Government was determined to restore military prestige first, it came increasingly to question the advantages of Confederation and in particular of Frere's implementation of it. Frere attempted to justify his position in a long letter to Sir Michael Hicks Beach at the Colonial Office – 'Few may now agree with my view as to the necessity of the suppression of the Zulu rebellion,' he wrote. 'Few, I fear, in this generation. But unless my countrymen are much changed, they will some day do me justice. I shall not leave a name to be permanently dishonoured.' Ironically, Frere's contemporaries were unimpressed, and indeed history has judged him on exactly those terms. In June 1879 Sir Garnet Wolseley was sent to southern Africa as a special commissioner with full civil and military powers. In effect he superseded both Frere and Chelmsford and behind his appointment was an implied criticism of both. With the change of administration in London from Conservative to Liberal Frere was recalled in August 1880. Frere vigorously argued his case on his return but his career was in ruins. He died in Wimbledon on 29 May 1884.

Fripp, Charles Edwin

Charles Fripp was born into a distinguished family of artists. His grandfather, Captain Nicholas Pocock, was a maritime artist, and his father, George Arthur Fripp, was a landscape painter. Fripp was born in Camden Town, London, on 4 September 1854. He studied at the Royal Academy of Munich and Nuremberg, and in 1875 took a post as a 'special artist' with the London illustrated paper, *The Graphic*. He was sent to southern Africa to cover the closing stages of the Eighth Cape Frontier War but, like most correspondents, left the Cape at the end of hostilities anticipating a more newsworthy conflict in Afghanistan. When news of Isandlwana reached London, the principle newspapers hastily dispatched their senior reporters back to Africa. Fripp arrived to cover the advance of the Eshowe Relief Column, and he was present at the Battle of kwaGingindlovu on 2 April.

During the second invasion he accompanied the advance of the 2nd Division and, with a number of other reporters, was present when the body of the Prince Imperial was discovered. He drew many sketches of the final advance to oNdini, and his drawings have a distinctive vitality and reflect the appearance of the different African groups he encountered with an unusual degree of accuracy. On 3 July he was sketching the return of Buller's mounted foray across the White Mfolozi drift when, with Zulu bullets splashing in the river nearby, Buller shouted at him to withdraw. Fripp – who was so preoccupied that he did not recognize Buller – expressed some indignation at being ordered to the rear like a defaulter when he was in fact a civilian. Lord William Beresford, riding past covered in the blood of a man he had saved in the skirmish, heard him, scolded him on his manners, and demanded an apology on Buller's behalf. Fripp refused to apologize and the two squared up to each other on the water's edge, exchanging punches until Fripp's fellow correspondents dragged him away. The following day he was inside Lord Chelmsford's square, sketching the Battle of Ulundi while lying on top of an ammunition cart – 'Now and again a bullet sighed overhead as I watched the beautiful advance of the enemy rapidly spreading over the undulations, disappearing and reappearing as the inequalities were traversed.' At the end of the war, he commented 'whatever rights and wrongs which brought on the war, these same brave Zulus died resisting an invasion of their country and homes. Naked savages as they were, let us honour them.'

After the war, Fripp continued his work as a war artist and covered the Transvaal Rebellion, campaigns in the American West, against the amaNdebele in Zimbabwe, in the Sudan, the Sino-Japanese War and in the Philippines. When resident in London he also served for thirteen years with the Artists' Rifles.

In 1885 Fripp exhibited a large oil-on-canvas painting of the Battle of Isandlwana at the Royal Academy in London. It is remarkable in that it is one of the few contemporary paintings of the Anglo-Zulu War executed by an artist who had experienced something of it. Although Fripp had been working intermittently on it for six years, it aroused little public interest at the time, largely because public attitudes to the war had changed in the years since the invasion. Ironically, however, the picture is now regarded as an iconic image of the Victorian Empire and is widely reproduced. It is arguably the most complex visual image to emerge from the war since the composition includes many typical elements of Victorian battle-painting – the central 'last stand', grouped around the colours, and the poignant juxtaposition of veteran sergeant and young drummer-boy – contrasted with background images which suggest the brutal reality of the fighting. It is also interesting to note that, unlike most examples of the genre, the picture foregrounds the experience of ordinary soldiers rather than officers. Fripp also produced a large colour study of the death of Lieutenants Melvill and Coghill which was reproduced as a supplement in *The Graphic*, and later a painting of the Battle of Tofrek in the Sudan campaign.

On 17 May 1901 Fripp married Louis Gertrude Renwick in the grounds of Porchester Castle, at the head of Portsmouth Harbour. The couple settled for a while in Porchester but Fripp then decided to join his brother Thomas in Canada to sketch the developing gold-rush. He died in Canada in 1906.

Gardner, Alan Coulston

Alan Gardner was born in 1846 and entered the Army as a cavalry officer, serving first in the 11th and then in the 14th Hussars. He passed out of the Staff College in 1872 and volunteered as a special service officer for the Zulu campaign. He was attached as a staff officer to Colonel Glyn's No. 3 column.

On 22 January he had accompanied Glyn under Lord Chelmsford's command to the hills at the head of the Mangeni valley, some twelve miles from the camp at Isandlwana. After inconsistent skirmishing during the morning, Chelmsford decided to order the remainder of the column to advance to join him, and Glyn sent Gardner back to Isandlwana with the order. Gardner arrived, however, just as reports reached the camp commander, Lieutenant Colonel Pulleine, that detachments of Colonel Durnford's force had discovered the Zulu army beyond the iNyoni heights. At first Pulleine seemed uncertain how to react until Gardner assured him that Chelmsford knew nothing of these developments. Gardner himself seems to have assisted in directing the movements of some of the mounted men during the battle.

When the British position collapsed he made his escape, crossing the Mzinyathi at Sothondose's Drift where he met Captain Essex and Lieutenant Cochrane. The three held a brief discussion and Gardner scribbled a hasty note of warning to the garrison at Rorke's Drift before all three rode to Helpmekaar. Essex and Cochrane stayed to help put the camp at Helpmekaar on a secure footing but Gardner rode on to Dundee to warn Wood's column of the disaster. At Dundee he found a volunteer to take his message to Utrecht. Later, Gardner's actions earned him the appreciation of his senior officers but an unfounded rumour that he might be rewarded with the Victoria Cross provoked a reaction among his colleagues in the field where a ditty was composed satirizing his exertions – 'I very much fear, that the Zulus are near, so hang it, I'm off to Dundee'. Gardner's senior officer on Glyn's staff, Major Clery, seems to have been responsible for some of the more unfavourable interpretations of his actions. When Chelmsford reorganized his forces after Isandlwana, Gardner was transferred as a staff officer to Colonel Wood. Wood also seems to have taken a dislike to him, although Gardner accompanied Colonel Buller's detachment during the assault on Hlobane Mountain on 28 March. Buller mentioned Gardner in dispatches and Gardner's horse was killed under him. He survived the disaster, however, and took part in the Battle of Khambula the following day, where he was wounded.

After the war, Gardner returned to Britain to take up a post as ADC to Lord Cowper, the Lord Lieutenant of Ireland. In 1885 he married Norah, daughter of Sir James Blyth, and the couple had two sons and two daughters.

Gardner developed a strong interest in big game hunting, travelling to India, Assam, Africa, North America and Australasia to shoot a representative cross-section of indigenous wildlife and his wife often accompanied him, 'herself shooting many wild animals'. On his retirement from the Army, with the rank of Colonel, Gardner became a JP and took an interest in politics. In 1895 he contested the East Marylebone constituency on behalf of the Liberals and in 1906 was elected for the Ross Division in Herefordshire. In the winter of 1907 he began to suffer from poor health and took a holiday in Gibraltar to recuperate. Here he suddenly succumbed to pneumonia and died in Algeçiras on Christmas Day, at the age of sixty-two. His body was brought home to England; in view of the controversy which surrounded his actions after Isandlwana, it is ironic that the inscription on his memorial in Stansted Mountfitchet churchyard, Essex, refers to 'Life's race well run'.

Glyn, Richard Thomas

Born 23 December 1831 in Meerut, India, Glyn was the only son of R.C. Glyn, an officer in the Honourable East India Company. On returning to England he enjoyed a conventional country upbringing which made him an expert horseman and a fanatical huntsman. Despite his short stature – he was just 5 feet 2 inches – Glyn was physically strong and keen to pursue a military career. When he was nineteen, his father purchased him a commission into the 82nd (Prince of Wales's Volunteers) Regiment, later the 2nd South Lancashires. After several years of duty in Ireland, Glyn and his regiment were sent to the Crimea and arrived on 2 September 1855, just six days before the fall of Sevastopol. They became part of the Army of Occupation until 1856 when Glyn married Anne Clements, the daughter of the former Colonel of the Royal Canadian Rifles. Their honeymoon period was cut short when Glyn's regiment was rushed to India to cope with the crisis of the Mutiny; the 82nd was part of Sir Colin Campbell's force that relieved the besieged force at Lucknow in mid-November 1857 and subsequently suffered in the fighting around Kanpur. Glyn was then promoted to captain and soon gained much experience in the hard and brutal suppression of the Mutiny.

Like many officers, Glyn found post-mutiny India an agreeable place to serve, particularly enjoying the opportunities to indulge his passion for hunting. Anne joined him and they set about producing a family of four daughters. He advanced up the promotion ladder by purchasing his majority in 1861. In 1867 he purchased the lieutenant colonelcy of the 1/24th Regiment, then stationed at Malta. In 1872 the regiment was transferred to Gibraltar, where Glyn was promoted to full colonel. Even here he was able to hunt across the border into Spain, which was about the only excitement to be had in this peaceful outpost.

After three pleasant but uneventful years the regiment was relieved to have a change of posting. At the end of November the Glyns and most of the 1/24th embarked on Her Majesty's

Troopship *Simoon* for Cape Town. Glyn's appearance at this time could be described as 'bristling'; with his full wax-tipped moustache and short aggressive-looking stature, he looked the archetypal irascible colonel. This appearance, however, belied his true personality. He had a steady and unflappable temperament, though somewhat unimaginative and lethargic. He was fortunate to command some very able officers, including Henry Pulleine who could be relied upon expertly to administer the regiment's day-to-day running.

In 1876 the 1/24th was ordered to the diamond diggings at Kimberley to counter unrest among the diggers. The march to Kimberley was long and arduous; keeping up a steady pace through the heat of the African days, the 1/24th took two months to cover the 700 miles. When they arrived, they found that their presence alone was enough to stifle the rebellion and there was little more to do than march all the way back to the Cape. Glyn returned to the delights of the hunt, where black-backed jackals served as the local equivalent of foxes. As Lieutenant Coghill of the 1/24th observed, 'the Colonel as good a little man as ever breathed has what amounts to monomania, 'unting being 'is 'obby.' Hunting may have had a particular masculine appeal to Glyn as an antidote to a family life dominated by his wife and daughters.

With the outbreak of the 9th Cape Frontier War in 1877 the 1/24th was ordered to the Transkei, and Glyn appointed commander, with the rank of colonel of the staff and brevet brigadier general. The campaign was a frustrating one of sweeps through the bush punctuated by occasional sharp fights. Nevertheless, the regiment had performed well and duly received the thanks of the Governor. Colonel Glyn received high praise from both the Duke of Cambridge and Sir Bartle Frere and, in a more tangible form of gratitude; he was made a Companion of the Bath.

In 1878, the 1/24th were ordered to Pietermaritzburg in Natal in preparation for the invasion of Zululand. With the political crisis deepening, Colonel Glyn bade farewell to his wife and daughters on 30 November and, to the accompaniment of the band, led his regiment out of Pietermaritzburg towards the desolate post of Helpmekaar to join the No.3 Column. Enduring constant heavy rain and deep mud, the Column took a week to cover the 100 miles to the Biggarsberg plateau. Glyn himself was appointed Column commander, although in the event his authority was largely superseded by Lord Chelmsford's decision to accompany the column in person. Glyn had a staff that were largely strangers to him and were newcomers to South Africa. His Principal Staff Officer was the contentious and egocentric Major Cornelius Clery, who had originally served in this capacity with Colonel Evelyn Wood's Number 4 Column (the Left Flank or Northern Column). He had been transferred at Lord Chelmsford's request, probably to ensure that the easy-going Glyn kept to his task. Clery, ever critical of his superiors, described Glyn as 'a guileless, unsuspicious man, very upright and scrupulously truthful, yet a slow, not to say lethargic temperament'. He undoubtedly was contrasting the relaxed unambitious Glyn with the energetic and talented Wood. When Chelmsford joined the column, tension developed between his staff and that of Colonel Glyn. Clery and Chelmsford's Military Secretary, Lieutenant Colonel John Crealock both lacked diplomacy but possessed vitriolic tongues which further strained relationships between the two camps. Crealock dismissed Glyn by saying, 'do not expect anything (of him). He is a purely regimental officer with no ideas beyond it.'

'Colonel Glyn and his staff were allowed to work the details – posting the guards, etc., and all the interesting work of that kind', commented Clery bitingly. In response, Glyn became disinterested and withdrawn. 'He (Glyn) was scarcely ever seen or heard of,' noted Clery, 'the more so as he got anything but encouragement to interest himself in what was going on'.

Throughout the coming campaign, Chelmsford treated Glyn with an air of impatience, brushing aside his suggestions that both Helpmekaar and Rorke's Drift be fortified. On the 12th, Glyn was nominally in command of the assault on inkosi Sihayo's homestead, although Chelmsford again accompanied the expedition. On arrival at Isandlwana on 20 January, Glyn gave the instructions for the layout of the camp but Chelmsford was reluctant to fortify it because of the practical difficulties involved. Following the encounter with Zulu forces at the head of the Mangeni gorge on the evening of the 21st, Chelmsford decided to advance at once and again offered Glyn nominal command of the force. Yet the main Zulu army was not where Chelmsford searched for it; that night he and Glyn and their men returned to the devastated field at Isandlwana. The following morning they returned to their starting point at Rorke's Drift. Pausing only to congratulate the defenders, Chelmsford and his staff rode off to Pietermaritzburg to report the disaster. Colonel Glyn, in a complete state of shock at the loss of his regiment, was left to fortify Rorke's Drift.

Fearing that the Zulus would attack at any time, Glyn had a strong perimeter built around the camp and the survivors slept inside each night. The lack of shelter from the incessant rain soon made the post insanitary, and it was plagued at night by false alarms. Glyn himself withdrew still further into his shell of despondency and took little interest in the misery around him. Without doubt he was displaying all the symptoms of a breakdown, grieving for his lost regiment and feeling guilty that he had survived. On 4 February a patrol from the fort discovered the Queen's Colour of the 1/24th, which had been lost during the retreat from Isandlwana. Glyn was moved to tears when the Colour was returned to him.

While the isolated Glyn was suffering both mentally and physically at Rorke's Drift, Lord Chelmsford and his staff attempted to play down their role in the disaster. Chelmsford suggested that Glyn 'was solely responsible' for the position of the camp, while admitting subtly 'that Colonel Glyn fully and explicitly accepted this responsibility cannot, however, affect the ultimate responsibility of the General-in-Command'. This attempt to implicate Glyn in the blame cut little ice with those who knew how limited the Colonel's authority actually was. Anne Glyn, recovering herself from the terrible news, was incensed at the attempts to blame her husband and was outspoken in her criticism of Chelmsford. Glyn himself seemed too numb to do more than briefly give the facts without comment to the Board of Enquiry. Chelmsford then turned his attention to Colonel Durnford as the conveniently dead scapegoat.

As the months passed, so reinforcements began to reach South Africa and Chelmsford could put his new invasion plans into effect. Glyn was appointed to command the First Infantry Brigade, which consisted of newly arrived reinforcements, and when the new advance began on 1 June they proved prone to false alarms. Indeed, the advance began badly when the Prince Imperial was killed in a skirmish; Glyn was appointed to the court martial, which tried the surviving officer, Lieutenant J. B. Carey. Although the reconstituted 1/24th was considered too unsteady and inexperienced to accompany the final assault on oNdini, Glyn himself was present inside the square during the battle on 4 July. For the 24th the war was over and the regiment began the long march back to Pietermaritzburg, where the Glyns were reunited. Then they travelled to the encampment at Pinetown, where Colonel Glyn had the pleasant duty of presenting the Victoria Cross to Surgeon Major James Reynolds (Rorke's Drift) and Lieutenant Edward Browne 1/24th (Khambula).

Finally, the 24th embarked on the troopship *Egypt* and set sail for England on 27 August; during the voyage the redoubtable Anne Glyn used her needlework skills to repair the tattered Queen's Colour. In May 1880 Glyn relinquished his command of the 1/24th and took charge of the Brigade Depot at Brecon. The following year, the regiment was given the new title of 'The South Wales Borderers'.

In 1882 Richard Glyn was promoted to major general and appointed a KCB. He eventually retired as a lieutenant general and lived at Mortimer in Berkshire. A sad and stooped little man, Glyn's remaining years were overshadowed by the memory of his lost family on the rocky slopes of Isandlwana. In 1898 he was honoured with the title of Colonel of the South Wales Borders. It was in this capacity that he saw off his old regiment as they went to South Africa again, this time to fight the Boers. Within a few months of their departure, he died on 21 November 1900 and was buried in the family grave at Ewell, Surrey.

Griffiths, William VC

Griffiths was born in Roscommon, Ireland, in 1841 and enlisted in the Army in Warwick on 16 April 1859. In 1867 he was serving as a member of the 2nd Battalion 24th Regiment, a party of which had been sent to the Andaman Islands in the Bay of Bengal to investigate the fate of sailors who were feared murdered by islanders. A detachment of soldiers was put ashore and was promptly attacked. They were stranded on the beach, and several attempts to evacuate them to a ship offshore failed due to the heavy surf. In the end they were saved, thanks to the determined effort of a surgeon and four men of the 24th who took a boat through the surf at great personal risk. All five men were awarded the Victoria Cross for gallantry (an unusual award since they were not actually engaged with the enemy at the time). Among them was Private Griffiths. Griffiths continued to serve with the battalion and was a member of G Company when the 2/24th was sent to the Cape at the end of the 9th Frontier War. The battalion was attached to the No. 3 Centre Column; on 22 January G Company remained in the camp at Isandlwana on picquet duty when the rest of the battalion marched to Mangeni under Lord Chelmsford. Griffiths was killed during the Zulu attack later that day; no details of his death have survived. His VC was acquired by the regiment at auction in the 1890s, having apparently been found on the battlefield – perhaps by a member of one of the burial details.

Hackett, Robert Henry

Hackett was the son of Thomas Hackett and his wife Jane of Riverstown, County Tipperary, Ireland. Robert Hackett's brothers Thomas and Charles were also distinguished soldiers; Thomas won the Victoria Cross during the Indian Mutiny and rose to the rank of colonel. Robert Hackett was commissioned as an ensign into the 90th (Perthshire) Light Infantry. In 1878 the 90th was dispatched to southern Africa to take part in the closing stages of the 9th Cape Frontier War, and Hackett served with them throughout the subsequent campaign. On the eve of the Anglo-Zulu War the battalion was marched overland to Utrecht, and attached to Colonel Wood's column. Hackett was by this time a brevet major. According to Wood – himself a 90th officer – Hackett was a likeable but conservative officer:

> ...decidedly old-fashioned, and I have now before me an indignant letter, written four years before his terrible wound, urging me to use my influence to stop what he regarded as the craze for interviewing officers such as himself, nearly forty years of age. He pointed out the injustice of expecting old dogs to learn these new tricks, and argued that as he had bought his commission without any liability to be examined for promotion, it was unjust to exact any such test from him now; and added that, as no Staff appointment would tempt him to leave the battalion, and it was generally admitted that he was efficient in all Regimental duties, all he wanted was to be left alone, and not troubled with books. He was, indeed, a good Regimental officer; he managed the Mess, the Canteen, and the Sports club, and, indeed, was a pillar of the Regiment. He kept a horse, but seldom, or never, rode, putting it generally at the disposal of the subalterns of his company. He played no games, and lived for nothing but the welfare of the men in his Company, and the reputation of the Regiment.

Hackett was present during Wood's foray against the abaQulusi at Zungwini Mountain on 24 January, when several companies of the 90th swept across the western foot of Hlobane.

On 29 March, during the attack on Khambula camp,

Hackett was present in the main wagon laager where the majority of the 90th was stationed. After the repulse of the Zulu right 'horn' in the early stages of the battle, the British position was threatened by the Zulu left, which assembled in the valley to the south of Khambula ridge, and which was able to advance close to the wagon laagers before coming under fire. Recognizing the threat from this direction, Colonel Wood ordered two companies of the 90th to sally from the laager and line the head of the slope, looking down into the valley. This sortie was led by Hackett. As they emerged from the protection of the laager into the open, these companies were exposed to a galling crossfire from Zulu marksmen ensconced among the rocks on either side of the slope; in particular, they were enfiladed by the fire from a number of marksmen – many armed with Martini-Henry rifles captured at Isandlwana – who had occupied a tall growth of grass and mealies which had sprouted from the camp's dung heaps lying to Hackett's right. Despite this, the companies 'marched out at a steady double', the subalterns running ahead of their men and directing them into position. Once they had deployed at the head of the slope, they were able to sweep the approaches below with volley fire, breaking up the Zulu concentrations and driving the left 'horn' further down the valley. They could not sustain this position for long, however, because of the fierce return fire which fell particularly heavily upon the exposed officers and NCOs, who moved about encouraging their men. Colour Sergeant Allen of the 90th was shot dead, Lieutenant Arthur Bright was shot through both thighs, and Hackett was struck in the head.

After a few minutes Wood ordered the sortie to withdraw, and – according to his obituary – Hackett's wound was so severe that it was assumed he was dead. A bullet had struck his right temple, passing through his head behind the eyes and emerging on the other side. Remarkably, the bullet caused no lasting damage to the brain or skull, but irrevocably destroyed both optic nerves.

When Hackett regained consciousness, he remained deeply

shocked. According to Wood:

> The morning after the action, he was a pitiable sight, for a bullet had passed from one temple to another, and, without actually hitting the eyes, had protruded the eyeballs, injuring the brain. He was unconscious of the terrible nature of his wounds, possibly from pressure on the brain, and observed to me 'your Commissariat officers are very stingy in not lighting up this Hospital tent; the place is in absolute darkness'. We were so fond of him that nobody ventured to tell him the truth, and it was not until he was in Maritzburg that the doctors begged a lady, who was a constant visitor to the Hospital, to break the news to him.

Hackett's wound inevitably rendered him unfit for further service. Once he had sufficiently recovered, he returned to Ireland where he lived in the care of his brother, Colonel Thomas Hackett, until the latter died shortly afterwards in a shooting accident. Robert Hackett died at Lockeen, near Riverstown, Co. Tipperary, on 30 December 1893.

Harford, Henry Charles

Harford was born in 1850. His father, Captain Charles Joseph Harford, was a captain in the 12th Lancers. In 1864 Captain Harford bought a tobacco estate at Pinetown in Natal and the family emigrated to southern Africa. Here Henry Harford spent a happy and adventurous boyhood, learned to ride and shoot, and discovered an interest in the natural world that would last throughout his life.

In 1870, the Harford family began to break up. Henry returned to England with the intention of joining the Army; in 1871 Captain Harford gave up farming for the chance of a greater fortune in Kimberley, where he died in 1874. One of Henry Harford's sisters married into the Natal settler gentry; his mother and remaining sisters returned to England.

Henry Harford entered the Army as an ensign in the 99th Regiment in 1870. His early years were spent on garrison duty in Ireland, but in 1877 the regiment was posted to Chatham, Kent, and Harford accepted the post as adjutant. In late 1878, the War Office requested volunteers for special service posts in Natal, the result of Chelmsford's preparations for invading Zululand. 'As I had spent most of my youth, seven years, in Natal,' recalled Harford, 'and had a very fair knowledge of the Kaffir language, it occurred to me that I should stand a very good chance of getting out if I put in an application.'

His application was accepted, and Harford resigned the adjutancy in favour of Lieutenant Arthur Davison. Ironically, the 99th was later ordered to Natal, and arrived just in time to join the invasion; Lieutenant Davison was to die at Eshowe during the siege.

Harford arrived in Durban on 2 December 1878, and was given the post of Staff Officer to the 3rd Regiment, Natal Native Contingent, which was then assembling at Sandspruit, near Helpmekaar, on the Mzinyathi border. Harford joined the regiment a few weeks before the invasion began. On 11 January, he led the 2nd Battalion across the border by means of a previously unknown drift a few hundred yards upstream from Rorke's Drift:

> The fog was so dense one could barely see anything a yard in front, but at last, after hugging the bank very closely for about half a mile or more, we came to a spot that looked worth a trial. So I put my pony at it and got across all right, the bed of the river being nice and hard; but the water came up to the saddle flaps, and there was a nasty bank to scramble up on the opposite side. However, that did not matter, it was good enough... [It] was subsequently known as Harford's Drift, but I don't suppose it has been used since...

The following day (12 January 1879) Harford accompanied the 2nd Battalion in the attack on *inkosi* Sihayo's stronghold. The 2nd Battalion arrived after the assault had begun, and in particular Harford noticed that a number of officers and

NCOs of the 1st Battalion were in difficulties, being engaged in the rocks at the foot of a line of cliffs, and having been largely deserted by their men. Harford ran over to assist. One of those officers, Major George Hamilton Browne, recalled Harford's arrival in an anecdote by which Harford is largely remembered today:

> He was a charming companion, one of the very best, but he was a crazy bug and beetle hunter, and would run about on the hottest day with a landing net to catch butterflies and other insects. He moreover collected and treasured snakes, scorpions and loathsome beasts of all sorts. He had never been under fire before and had on two or three occasions talked to me about a man's feelings while undergoing his baptism of fire, and expressed hopes he would be cool and good while undergoing his. Well we were in rather a hot corner and he was standing to my right rear when I heard an exclamation, and turning round saw him lying on the ground having dropped his sword and revolver. 'Good God, Harford', I said, 'you are hit!' 'No, Sir,' he replied, 'not hit but I have caught such a beauty.' And there the lunatic, in his first action, and under heavy fire, his qualms of nervousness all forgotten, had captured some infernal microbe or other, and was blowing its wings out, as unconscious of the bullets striking the rocks all round him as if he had been in his garden at home ...

Reminded of his priorities, Harford noticed that the NNC was suffering heavily from a group of Zulu snipers concealed in a cave further up the slope. Harford decide to clear them out, working his way up through the boulders and corpses of Zulus killed in the fighting, until he reached the opening of the cave. Here he was shocked to find a Zulu squatting in the entrance, 'his head showed above the rock, and his wide-open eyes glared at me; but I soon discovered that he was dead'. Suddenly another Zulu emerged from the gloom, pointed his musket at Harford's face and fired – but the cap snapped, and the Zulu threw down the gun and rushed backwards, Harford blazing away at him ineffectually with his revolver. Harford promptly called over his shoulder to an NCO of the contingent who was nearby, to follow him into the cave, but the man merely called to the troops below 'Captain Harford is killed!' 'No he's not,' shouted Harford in frustration, 'he is very much alive!' Entering the cave, Harford called out in Zulu and persuaded four men hiding there to surrender, ushering them out at the point of his empty revolver. The capture was carried out in sight of Chelmsford's staff and earned him a commendation – although it is interesting to note that a similar deed, accomplished by two of Evelyn Wood's staff at Hlobane on 28 March, resulted in the award of two Victoria Crosses.

At dawn on the 21st Harford accompanied the sweep under Major Dartnell of the Malakatha and Hlazakazi heights. During the following night, after the encounter at the Mangeni gorge, the 3rd NNC gave way to nervousness, and Harford spent much of the night rounding up runaways and returning them to the bivouac. The following morning, once Dartnell's command had been reinforced by Lord Chelmsford's detachment from Isandlwana, the NNC swept across Magogo hill, dispersing small parties of Zulus who had remained there overnight. Harford again came under fire from a Zulu marksman concealed among the rocks, and 'I quickly shot at him. I then went after him, and, crawling on all fours, found him badly wounded, with a dead Zulu lying close to him.'

That evening, the 3rd NNC returned with Chelmsford's force to find the camp at Isandlwana devastated. Looking for the NNC officers' tents, Harford found that they had gone but between them 'lay the bodies of two artillerymen, disembowelled and terribly mutilated'. Again attempting to secure the wavering NNC, Harford went round after dark to ensure the men had not deserted their places, 'and many of the dark figures I ran up against, who were not squatting, I feel certain were Zulus and not our men'.

The following morning Chelmsford's command returned to Rorke's Drift. The men of the 3rd NNC were disbanded, but the officers, including Harford, were mostly to remain at the ruined mission for several months; Harford spent his time between Helpmekaar and Rorke's Drift and he was given custody of both Captain Stevenson and Lieutenant Higginson who were placed under arrest following their activities on the day of the battle.* With all tents lost at Isandlwana, in cramped and insanitary conditions made worse by the presence of undiscovered Zulu dead nearby and by nightly downpours – a 'terrible state of things, living in such slush' – nerves were frayed and morale deteriorated. Hamilton Browne recalls that Harford's enthusiasm for naturalism was undiminished, however, and that he took to preserving his specimens in the officers' gin supply:

> He was such a good fellow and soon forgiven, but I do not think the dear fellow ever quite understood what an awful sin he had committed or realized what a wicked waste of liquor he had perpetrated.

Gradually, as no Zulu counter-attack materialized, British self-confidence returned and a number of patrols were mounted along the border. On 4 February a group of NNC officers, including Harford, and led by Major Wilsone Black, 24th, rode as far as Sothondose's (Fugitives') Drift, and found the bodies of Lieutenants Melvill and Coghill, killed during the rout after Isandlwana. It had been widely reported that Melvill had been attempting to save the Queens Colour of the 1/24th, and Black's party searched the bodies, but to no avail. They then descended to the river, where Harford spotted the Colour pole sticking up among the rocks. Captain Harbour of the NNC waded in and recovered it, pulling up the tattered silk which had been jammed among the boulders. Harford carried the Colour back to Rorke's Drift in triumph; 'I very much doubt whether such another case has ever occurred that an officer on duty and belonging to another Regiment has been given the honour of carrying the Queen's Colour.'

In April, Harford rejoined the 99th Regiment which,

following the relief of Eshowe, had returned to the Thukela camps. Lieutenant Davison was dead, and Harford resumed the adjutancy. The 99th was then attached to the 1st Division and saw no further fighting, although Harford, acting as interpreter, joined one of the patrols sent out to search for the furtive King Cetshwayo. Although the patrol was not successful, it did visit the homestead of *inkosi* Somkhele kaMalanda, the head of the powerful Mpukonyoni section, who lived in the northern coastal plain. With the war all but over, Somkhele was friendly enough, but offered no clues as to the whereabouts of the king. Harford was greeted by a warrior keen to swap stories of the Isandlwana campaign, who 'showed me eleven wounds that he had received, bounding off in the greatest ecstasy to show how it all happened'. Shortly after returning to camp, Harford was present when King Cetshwayo was brought in by Major Marter's patrol, 'with a proud and dignified air and grace, looking a magnificent specimen of his race and every inch a warrior in his grand *umutcha* of leopard skin and tails, with lion's teeth and claw charms around his neck'.

The capture of the king effectively spelt the end of the campaign, but ironically Harford would see him again. The 99th was sent from Natal to Bermuda, but with the outbreak of the Transvaal Rebellion in 1881 returned to the Cape. Although it did not take part in the fighting, the regiment was quartered on the Cape Flats, not far from the farm Oude Moulen, where Cetshwayo was then quartered. The king was regularly invited to attend functions at the 99th's mess, and Harford noted that he 'always took the greatest interest in inspecting the Band instruments and hearing the different sounds that were got out of them'.

Harford remained with the 99th Regiment, serving in Malta and India, rose to the rank of colonel, and at various times commanded both battalions, but saw no further active service, being deemed by a medical board to be both physically and mentally unfit for active command. In 1898 he married Florence Page, and together they had one child, Violet Eva.

117

From 1902 to 1905 he commanded the 62nd Regimental District in the UK, and from 1905 he was Colonel in Charge of Records for the Yorkshire Grouped Regimental Districts. In 1907 he was made a Commander of the Bath. He retired to Sussex and died on 25 March 1937.

*Captain Stevenson and his NNC abandoned Rorke's Drift prior to the Zulu attack and Lieutenant Higginson was suspected of desertion from Isandlwana and stealing a trooper's horse to effect his escape. The trooper, Trooper Barker, survived and was later recommended for the VC by Colonel Wood. Both officers were arrested at Helpmekaar on the orders of Commandant Lonsdale and given into the custody of Harford. Stephenson was returned to Rorke's Drift the following day and dismissed. Higginson was temporarily able to explain away his actions and was released.

Harness, Arthur

Harness was born in Woolwich on 2 June 1838, the son of Lieutenant (later General) Sir Henry Drury Harness of the Royal Engineers and his wife Caroline. Caroline Harness died nine days after Arthur's birth, leaving four children of which Arthur was the youngest of two sons. He was educated at Carshalton and the Royal Military Academy at Woolwich and entered the Royal Artillery in 1857. He was posted to the 3rd Battery 13th Company RA in Malta and remained there for five years. Between 1861 and 1872 he served with various batteries in England, Ireland and India. He was promoted second captain in 1868 and captain in 1872. In 1877 he was appointed major and given command of N Battery 5th Brigade which in January 1878 was sent to the Cape. The battery took part in the closing stages of the 9th Frontier War (Harness' first active service) including the sweeps of the Perie Bush and the attack on the Xhosa refuge at Intaba-ka-Ndonda.

At the close of the Frontier campaign N/5 battery was sent to the Zulu border and attached to the No. 3 (Centre) Column. Harness was promoted brevet lieutenant colonel on 24

118

December 1878 and under his command the battery covered the crossing of the Mzinyathi River on 11 January 1879. Early on the morning of 22 January, Harness was ordered to take four of the battery's six guns with the force sent to the Mangeni hills under Lord Chelmsford's command. The guns lagged behind the advance due to the difficult nature of the ground; at one point, on receiving a report that the camp at Isandlwana was under attack, Harness turned the guns about but was ordered by Chelmsford's staff to resume the march. When Chelmsford's command returned to Isandlwana that evening Harness was ordered to shell the camp to drive out any Zulus who might have remained there.

On 24 January, at Helpmekaar, Harness was given command of a court of inquiry set up by Lord Chelmsford to examine 'the loss of the camp'. The purpose of the court was specific and limited and the findings were intended for Lord Chelmsford's use, and as a result Harness discarded a good deal of evidence which he did not consider significant to his remit – much to the frustration of historians since. Harness continued to serve throughout the war, and N/5 Battery was attached to the 2nd Division; Harness was present at the Battle of Ulundi. The battery was then attached to Colonel Baker Russell's column during the pacification operations in northern Zululand.

Harness left Zululand in October 1879 and was awarded the CB on his return to England by Queen Victoria. He was destined to see no further active service but remained an ardent supporter of Lord Chelmsford. When the journalist Archibald Forbes' attacked Chelmsford's conduct of the war in *The Nineteenth Century* magazine Harness responded in *Fraser's Magazine* in April 1880.

In December 1881 Harness was appointed to the captaincy of a company of gentleman cadets at Woolwich with the rank of colonel. From 1889 to 1894 he was an extra ADC to the Duke of Cambridge. From 1892 to 1894 he commanded the RA in the North-Eastern District. In 1894 he was promoted major general and he retired in 1897, although he held

119

honorary appointments until his death in Brighton on 13
October 1927. He remained unmarried.

Harrison, Richard

Harrison was born on 26 May 1837, the second son of the
Reverend B. J. Harrison. He was educated at Harrow with no
intention of a military career but, when the War Office posted
an advert offering direct commissions to public schoolboys in
the aftermath of the early losses in the Crimea, his headmaster
volunteered Harrison. He attended the Royal Military
Academy at Woolwich and entered the Royal Engineers on 31
July 1855. He was promptly sent to the Crimea, but the war
was over by the time he arrived. Instead, he went to India and
took part in a number of operations around Lucknow, in
Rohilkund, in the final operation in Awahd and in the pursuit
of the Nana Sahib.

In 1859 he served in the China expedition and was present in
the attack on the Dagu Forts; he was attached to the
Quartermaster-General's staff and was awarded a brevet
majority. In the 1860s he was posted to Canada and took the
opportunity to travel in America to see something of the Civil
War; on one occasion he was mistaken for a spy and nearly
hanged. He returned to an appointment in Aldershot, married
in 1870 (the couple had four children), was promoted brevet
lieutenant colonel and, on his second attempt, passed through
Staff College. On the outbreak of the Zulu War he was sent to
Natal as a RE company officer with reinforcements after
Isandlwana. On arrival, however, he was transferred to the
Headquarters Staff as Assistant Quartermaster-General. As
such he was largely responsible for selecting the route of
invasion for the 2nd Division and throughout May he
organized a number of long-range patrols into Zulu territory,
feeling for the Zulu positions and looking for a viable road. He
commanded several of these himself. Attached to his staff was
Louis Napoleon, the exiled French Prince Imperial. The
Prince's exuberance on several occasions placed him in danger,
and Harrison was ordered to confine him to desk work in

camp. On 1 June – the day appointed for the 2nd Division advance – the Prince was keen to see something of the troop movements and Harrison, aware that the country ahead had been thoroughly scouted and pronounced free of Zulus, relented. In the event the Prince's patrol strayed far ahead of the British advance and was ambushed; Louis himself was killed. Harrison found himself embroiled in the recriminations that followed. He was not censured and continued to serve throughout the remainder of the war. At the end of the Zulu campaign, with British attention now shifting to the Transvaal, Harrison was given the task of scouting the stronghold of the baPedi king, Sekhukhune, and he served throughout that expedition in late 1879. In 1880 he returned to a post at Aldershot; in 1882 he served in Egypt and in 1884 was in charge of the lines of communications during Wolseley's Gordon Relief Expedition, but was invalided home.

He occupied a number of appointments in the UK, and in July 1888 was promoted major general. In 1889 he became Governor of the Royal Military Academy at Sandhurst and was awarded the KCB. A number of other home appointments followed and he retired in 1903, after forty-nine years' service, with the rank of major general. He died at his home in Brixham, Devon, in 1931 at the age of ninety-four.

Hart, Arthur Fitzroy

Fitzroy Hart – as he was usually known – was born in 1844, one of several sons of H. G. Hart, a career soldier who rose to the rank of lieutenant general. Fitzroy Hart was educated at Cheltenham and entered the 31st Regiment at the age of twenty; a number of his brothers also had distinguished military careers.

He married in 1868 and the couple had four children, two boys and two girls. In 1872 he passed through Staff College and the following year accompanied Sir Garnet Wolseley's expedition to Asante, in West Africa, as a 'special service' officer. He was employed in Russell's Regiment, which was composed of locally-raised auxiliaries, and commanded the

Sierra Leone company throughout the war. He was present at the actions of Amoaful and Ordashu and the capture of Kumase, and was slightly wounded in skirmishing. At the end of the campaign he was attached to the Quartermaster General's Department, and mapped the Cape Castle coast. In November 1878 he again volunteered as a 'special service' officer for Lord Chelmsford's imminent invasion of Zululand and was attached to the 2nd Regiment, Natal Native Contingent, as staff officer with the rank of captain. The 2nd NNC was part of Pearson's coastal column, and Hart was with the regiment from the start of the invasion. On 22 January detachments from his command were scouting the slopes of Wombane hill, beyond the Nyezane River, when they blundered into the vanguard of a Zulu army, commanded by Godide kaNdlela, concealed on the heights beyond. The encounter provoked a Zulu attack, and in the confusion several officers and NCOs of the NNC were killed. Hart himself narrowly escaped being cut off and killed with the rest. At the height of the battle, the Zulu centre occupied a deserted homestead lying across the road. Hart was ordered to clear the way but the men of the NNC refused to accompany him. Instead he led the regiment's white NCOs who advanced up the slope firing volleys until they reached the homestead. Their advance was later supported by the Naval Brigade, but Hart, on horseback, was first among the Zulus who then gave way and retreated. The following day Pearson occupied the abandoned mission station at Eshowe. This had been designated as a forward supply depot, and Pearson ordered it to be entrenched; much of the initial manual labour fell to the 2nd NNC, and Hart personally directed their efforts.

When news of the defeat at Isandlwana reached the garrison, however, Pearson decided to reduce his force and most of the 2nd NNC, including Hart, were sent back to the Thukela. They remained in garrison there until the end of March, when Lord Chelmsford assembled a force to relief Eshowe. Hart accompanied the new advance and took part in the decisive battle at kwaGingindlovu on 2 April, where he was mentioned in dispatches. After the relief of Eshowe, he continued to serve in the coastal theatre, and was brigade major of the 2nd Brigade of the 1st Division. He ended the war as the Principal Staff Officer with Clarke's column.

In 1881 he returned to southern Africa as Deputy Acting Adjutant and Quartermaster General to Sir Evelyn Wood during the closing stages of the Transvaal Rebellion. In 1882 he was attached to the Intelligence Department during the Egyptian expedition, and he was slightly wounded at Kassassin, and present at Tel-el-Kebir. He was promoted lieutenant colonel. Between 1891 and 1895 he commanded the 1st Battalion East Surreys in India. He returned to Britain for appointments in Belfast and Aldershot and, in 1899, was sent to southern Africa again as a major general commanding the Irish Brigade. He served under Buller during the first ill-fated attempts to relieve Ladysmith.

During the Battle of Colenso (15 December 1899) Hart's brigade famously advanced in close formation into a loop in the Thukela River, and suffered heavy casualties as a result. Hart's personal courage was unquestionable but he believed in the moral effect of a conspicuous attack in good order and – like many of his generation – had failed to realize that the widespread use of magazine rifles and smokeless powder had made such tactics dangerously obsolete. He was known to his men as 'No-Bobs Hart' – a sly reference both to his admonition that his men should not duck under fire ('No bobbing!') and a sharp comment on his capabilities in comparison with the popular Lord Roberts (who was known as 'Bobs'). Nevertheless, Hart was a competent and energetic officer and, when later transferred to the Orange Free State, he was responsible for the relief of Colonial troops besieged by the Boers in the town of Wepener.

In 1902 Hart added his wife's maiden name to his own by Royal Licence, becoming Arthur Fitzroy Hart-Synnot. He retired from the Army in 1904 and died on 20 April 1910.

Harward, Henry Hollingworth

Henry Harward was born in Sevenoaks, Kent, on 25 November 1847. He entered the British Army as an ensign in the 1st West India Regiment in December 1871. Like Jahleel Carey, he may have been motivated in his choice of regiment by the higher standard of living colonial regiments afforded the less well off. In 1873 he took part in Sir Garnet Wolseley's influential Asante campaign in West Africa, during which time he was adjutant of two British forts on the coast in succession. At the end of the Asante campaign he transferred into the 80th Regiment (Staffordshire Volunteers). He served in China, and was present as a lieutenant when the battalion was sent to southern Africa in 1877. In October 1878 the 80th took part in the ill-fated expedition against the BaPedi of King Sekhukhune, where Harward was noted for having led a patrol which successfully destroyed a quantity of Pedi crops. With the outbreak of the Zulu campaign, the 80th were attached to Colonel Hugh Rowlands' column, operating on the Transvaal/Swazi border.

On 6 February Harward, commanding C Company, was among a detachment of the 80th which arrived at the German settlement of Lüneburg, on the exposed Phongolo frontier. This detachment was supplied by convoys which originated in the Transvaal and marched via Rowlands' base at Derby. At the end of February, a convoy of eighteen wagons, carrying food and ammunition, set out from the Transvaal. No escort was provided as it was considered safe until it reached the vicinity of Lüneburg. On 1 March, Major Charles Tucker, commanding the 80th at Lüneburg, dispatched D Company to meet the wagons and escort them in. Owing to a misunderstanding, however, D Company returned to Lüneburg a few days later, abandoning the convoy on the road. The wagons were then on the road a few miles from Meyer's Drift on the Ntombe; although almost within sight of Lüneburg, this was the most vulnerable stretch of the road since it ran close to the Tafelberg stronghold of the guerrilla leader, Prince Mbilini waMswati.

On 7 March Captain David Moriarty of the 80th was sent by Tucker with a company-sized detachment to collect the convoy. By the 9th, he had assembled the wagons on the north bank of the Ntombe, but heavy rain had swollen the river and it was impossible to get all but two of the wagons across. Further rain prevented any activity on the 11th, and on the 12th Tucker, growing concerned as to the convoy's safety, rode out from Lüneburg to assess the situation. Lieutenant Harward went with him. After urging Moriarty to bring in the wagons as quickly as possible, Tucker returned to Lüneburg leaving Harward at the drift with Moriarty's party. Harward later rode out with several men to gather up cattle that had strayed, and returned to the camp just before dark. He went to Moriarty's tent and fell asleep, but Moriarty later woke him and ordered him to cross by an improvised raft to take command of the party on the other bank. Harward did so, and again went to sleep; there were thirty-four men on his side of the river, including an experienced NCO, Sergeant Anthony Booth. With the darkness came a return of the rain that only eased in the small hours, giving way to a mist rising off the river.

At about 4 a.m., a single shot broke the silence from beyond the camp. Harward roused his detachment and sent across to Moriarty, asking for instructions; Moriarty told them to stand down but remain dressed with their pouches on. Shortly afterwards, Harward heard a sentry on the far bank shout 'Guard turn out', and emerging from his tent, through breaks in the mist, saw a body of warriors descending on the camp on Moriarty's side. The stranded convoy had proved too tempting a target for Prince Mbilini.

Harward stood his own men to and ordered them to lie under the wagons, firing across the river to drive back the attackers as best they could. Moriarty and his men, stumbled out of their tents cold, wet, half-dressed and half asleep. Most were cut down, and the survivors rushed into the river with the Zulus in pursuit. Harward did his best to direct his fire to cover the retreat, but as the Zulus began to cross the river in large numbers, according to his own account, they:

> ... fell upon our men, who already being broken, gave way, and a hand-to-hand fight ensued. I endeavoured to rally my men, but they were much too scattered, and finding reformation impossible, I mounted my horse and galloped to Lüneburg at utmost speed and reported all that had taken place.

It was left to Sergeant Booth and a Lance Corporal Burgess to rally a handful of men and try to cover the retreat of those on foot who remained. Booth was laconic in his description of Harward's actions – 'Lieutenant Harward saddled his horse and galloped away leaving us to do the best we could'.

Harward rode straight to Major Tucker and woke him looking, according to Tucker, 'the picture of death, on his knees ... he then fell onto my bed in a faint'. Tucker immediately gathered what mounted men he could and rode out to the Ntombe. Near the site he found Booth's party, retiring in good order; by the time he reached the drift, however, the Zulus had retired, leaving the bodies of Moriarty's men strewn in the debris of the wrecked and looted camp.

Over sixty men were killed alongside Moriarty, together with Civil Surgeon Cobbin and several civilian wagon drivers. Sergeant Booth was later awarded the Victoria Cross for his gallantry.

It is interesting to note that there must have been considerable sympathy for Harward among Tucker and the other officers of the 80th as he returned to his duties and served throughout the remainder of the campaign. Nevertheless, he does not appear to have taken an active part with those companies who joined the advance on oNdini or the subsequent operations against Sekhukhune.

On 12 February the 80th arrived at Pietermaritzburg after some of the most gruelling service undertaken by any of the infantry battalions in southern Africa. It was at this point – on

14 February, eleven months after the attack at Ntombe – that Henry Harward was placed under arrest, charged with misbehaviour before the enemy on that occasion. The charge seems to have been instigated by General Sir Garnet Wolseley who, not having been present in the early stages of the Anglo-Zulu War, and having no personal experience of the demoralization which occurred in the aftermath of Isandlwana, was determined to make examples of derelictions of duty which had occurred under Chelmsford's command.

Harward's trial took place between the 20 and 27 February. There were two accusations to defend; that he had failed to take proper precautions for the defence of the Ntombe camp, and that he had deserted his men under attack. The main line of Harward's defence was that he had only arrived at the drift on the day before the attack, and was not responsible for the provisions – or lack of them – Moriarty had already made. He had reacted to the first suggestion of an enemy presence, the gunshot in the night, but had then returned to his tent on Moriarty's orders. When the attack occurred, he had controlled his men well, and indeed in his official report of the incident Lord Chelmsford himself had commended Harward's handling of the party on the south bank. Only when his command disintegrated did Harward – the only man with a horse – ride off to raise the alarm. The court found him not guilty and ordered him to return to his duties.

When the findings were passed to Wolseley for confirmation, however, he was appalled at the implication:

That a Regimental Officer who is the only Officer present with a party of men actually and seriously engaged with the enemy, can, under any pretext whatever, be justified in deserting them, and by doing so abandoning them to their fate. The more helpless a position in which an officer finds his men, the more is his bounden duty to stay and share their fortune, whether for good or ill.

The Commander-in-Chief of the British Army, the Duke of

Cambridge, agreed with Wolseley, and ordered that a General Order criticizing Harward's conduct be read out at the head of every regiment.

Under such circumstances, it was clearly impossible for Harward to carry out his duties, and he resigned his commission on 11 May. He returned to England and to the obscurity of civilian life; his last recorded occupation was that of 'gentleman'. He died in St Leonards on 10 August 1897 at the age of forty-seven and is buried in Hastings Cemetery.

Hitch, Frederick VC

Frederick Hitch was born on 29 November 1856 in Edmonton, London, the son of John and Sara Hitch. He worked as a bricklayer's labourer before enlisting in the Army at Westminster Police Court on 7 March 1877.

He was posted to the 2nd Battalion 24th Regiment and enrolled in B Company. He was present with the battalion when it was sent to the Cape in February 1878 to take part in the closing stages of the 9th Cape Frontier War. B Company was present in the skirmishes around Intaba-ka-Ndoda and in the Perie Bush. At the end of 1878 the battalion was ordered to Natal to join the No. 3 (Centre) Column for the invasion of Zululand. When the Column crossed the Mzinyathi River into Zululand on 11 January 1879, B Company was left to guard the Drift and supply depot which had been established at the mission station at Rorke's Drift. Shortly after noon on the 22nd the camp of the Centre Column at Isandlwana was attacked and overrun by the Zulus; at about 4.30 p.m. the post at Rorke's Drift came under attack from elements of the Zulu reserve, who had crossed the Mzinyathi River. Private Hitch was ordered by Lieutenant Bromhead to climb onto the storehouse roof to watch for the Zulu advance; he gave a warning as they approached then scrambled down to take up a position in front of the hospital. This area was repeatedly assaulted by the Zulus and the defenders driven back; Hitch took part in the fierce bayonet fighting. After the defenders withdrew to the area in front of the storehouse, Hitch was one of a small group under Lieutenant Bromhead who defended an exposed angle, between the biscuit-box barricade and the front wall. Hitch was struggling with a Zulu attacking him from the front when he saw another warrior present his musket at him; he was unable to dodge and was hit in the shoulder. The ball shattered his right shoulder blade. Bromhead helped Hitch bind his useless arm with his waist-belt, and a comrade later bandaged the wound with the lining of a coat. For a while Hitch continued to fight, firing Bromhead's revolver with his left hand. When this became too painful, he took up packets of ammunition and distributed them among the defenders. He eventually passed out from exhaustion and loss of blood but regained consciousness the following morning, after the battle was over.

His injury was so severe that he was sent home and was treated at Netley Hospital. Bromhead recommended him for the award of the Victoria Cross, and this was presented to him at Netley on 12 August 1879. He was deemed unfit for further service, however, and discharged from the Army on 25 August 1879. He returned to London where he found work in the Corps of Commissionaires.

He married Emily Meurisse in July 1880 and the couple had six children. In February 1901 a thief took Hitch's VC from his commissionaires' uniform, and he applied for a replacement; he was eventually presented with another by Lord Roberts in September 1908. Hitch established a small transport business in south London and, with the advent of motor transport, secured a job as a taxi driver with the General Motor Cab Company in Chiswick. He died of pleuro-pneumonia and heart failure on 13 January 1913. He was buried with full military honours in Chiswick Old Cemetery in a ceremony attended by over 1,000 London cabbies.

Hook, Alfred Henry VC

Hook was the son of Henry Hook, an agricultural labourer, and his wife Ellen. He was born in Churcham, Gloucestershire, on 6 August 1850 and was baptised with the name Alfred; in adult life, however, he often used his father's name, Henry, and generally preferred to be known as Harry. As a youth he followed his father's profession – labourer and woodcutter – and in May 1869 he enlisted in the Royal Monmouthshire Militia.

On 26 December 1870 he married Comfort Jones, and the couple had three children. They lived with Comfort's parents and the claustrophobic conditions probably exaggerated tensions within the marriage; in March 1877 Hook left home and enlisted (under the name Henry) in Monmouth in the regular Army. He was enrolled in B Company of the 2nd Battalion 24th Regiment. In February 1878 the battalion was sent to the Cape to take part in the final suppression of Xhosa resistance at the end of the 9th Cape Frontier War. B Company took part in the skirmishing around the Xhosa strongholds of Intaba-ka-Ndoda and the Perie Bush. At the end of 1878 the battalion was attached to the No. 3 (Centre) Column for the invasion of Zululand. When the Column crossed into Zululand at Rorke's Drift on 11 January 1879 B Company was left to guard the Drift and supply depot which had been established in the mission buildings. Shortly after noon on 22 January the Column was attacked and the camp at Isandlwana overrun; at about 4. 30 p.m. elements from the Zulu reserve crossed the Mzinyathi River and attacked the post at Rorke's Drift. Hook was one of six able-bodied men posted in the hospital building – the old mission house – to guard the patients. He left one of the most graphic accounts of the battle to have emerged from a private soldier in which he described the desperate and brutal hand-to-hand struggle in the small, gloomy smoke-filled rooms and related how the defenders had to evacuate the patients by knocking holes through the interior walls. Hook survived the battle despite a scalp wound from a flung spear. After the battle, B Company remained encamped, together with the survivors of the Centre Column, in the squalid and insanitary conditions which prevailed at Rorke's Drift. Although they were later moved from the mission station to a new fort, constructed above the Drift and named

Fort Melvill, B Company remained in the vicinity until the end of the war.

Hook was nominated by his company commander, Lieutenant (later Major) Bromhead, for the Victoria Cross as early as 15 February and was presented with the award by Sir Garnet Wolseley at Fort Melvill on 3 August 1879 – the only one of the defenders to receive the award close to the site of the battle.

At the end of the war the 2/24th, including B Company, were sent to Gibraltar but here Hook, whose health had suffered due to the rigors of the campaign, decided to purchase his discharge. He left the Army on 25 June 1880 and returned to England. There is no truth in the popular story that Comfort Hook had believed him dead and re-married in his absence but the marriage was clearly beyond repair.

In 1881 Hook was working as a servant to a doctor in Monmouth but later that year he moved to London. He found work initially as a builders' labourer but was sent by chance to work at the British Museum. This resulted in a series of appointments at the museum which lasted throughout his career.

In June 1895 Comfort Hook – who had had little or no contact with her husband since he joined the regular Army – remarried. The couple were not at that time divorced and when Hook heard of it he had the marriage formally dissolved. On 10 April 1897 Hook married Ada Taylor and the couple had two children.

Throughout his time at the British Museum Hook retained his interest in military life and joined the 1st (Volunteer) Battalion of the Royal Fusiliers, rising to the rank of sergeant. His job brought him into constant contact with educated members of the public where the VC ribbon on his attendant's tunic aroused considerable interest; he was interviewed many times, became adept at telling the story of Rorke's Drift, and indeed became one of the best-known private soldiers of his day. He was suffering from the effects of tuberculosis and in January 1905 he reluctantly retired from his post at the museum. He returned to his native Gloucestershire but died on 12 March 1905. He was buried with full military honours in Churcham graveyard.

Jones, Robert VC

Robert Jones was born near Raglan, Monmouthshire, on 19 August 1857, the son of a farm labourer. He enlisted in the Army in Monmouth on 10 January 1876. He was posted to the 2nd Battalion 24th Regiment and enrolled in B Company. He was present with the battalion when it was sent to the Cape in February 1878 to take part in the closing stages of the 9th Cape Frontier War. B Company was present in the skirmishes around Intaba-ka-Ndoda and in the Perie Bush.

At the end of 1878 the battalion was ordered to Natal to join the No. 3 (Centre) Column for the invasion of Zululand. When the Column crossed the Mzinyathi River into Zululand on 11 January 1879 B Company was left to guard the Drift and supply depot which had been established at the mission station at Rorke's Drift. Shortly after noon on the 22nd the camp of the Centre Column at Isandlwana was attacked and overrun by the Zulus. At about 4.30 p.m. the post at Rorke's Drift came under attack from elements of the Zulu reserve, who had crossed the Mzinyathi River. Robert Jones was one of six able-bodied men posted to defend the hospital building. Once the Zulus had broken into the building, the defenders fought from room to room, knocking holes in the interior partitions and dragging the patients after them; Jones received three slight stomach wounds from spear-thrusts during the fighting. He was nominated by Lieutenant Bromhead for the Victoria Cross; the award was gazetted on 2 May 1879 and presented by Sir Garnet Wolseley on 11 September 1879.

After the war he continued to serve in B Company which was posted to Gibraltar and India. He returned to England in November 1881 and passed onto the Army Reserve. He was recalled for service briefly in 1882 and finally discharged from Army service in January 1888. He married Elizabeth Hopkins on 7 January 1885 and they subsequently had five children.

They settled in Peterchurch, Herefordshire, where Jones secured work as a groundsman for a retired officer, Major de la Hay. In later years he suffered recurring headaches, apparently the result of an injury he suffered 'near the eye'. The cause of this injury remains obscure and if it was inflicted at Rorke's Drift it is not mentioned on Jones' medical report. On 6 September 1898, while at work, he borrowed his employer's gun and said he was going to shoot crows. Shortly afterwards a shot was heard and Jones was found lying dead. He had shot himself through the mouth. An inquest declared that he had committed suicide while of an unsound mind. His headaches seem to have been the immediate cause of his depression but it is highly probable he was still suffering from post-traumatic stress dating to his experiences at Rorke's Drift. He was forty-one years old; he was buried in Peterchurch.

Jones, William VC

William Jones was born in Evesham, Worcestershire, in 1839 – although there is a family tradition he was born in Bristol – the son of James Jones, a builder's labourer. He worked as a boot closer before enlisting in the Army on 21 December 1858. He was enrolled in the 2/24th Regiment and served in Mauritius, Burma and India.

In May 1875 he married Elizabeth Goddard. He became a member of B Company, 2/24th Regiment and both he and his wife accompanied the battalion when it was sent to the Cape in February 1878 to take part in the closing stages of the 9th Cape Frontier War. B Company was present in the skirmishes around Intaba-ka-Ndoda and in the Perie Bush. At the end of 1878 the battalion was ordered to Natal to join the No. 3 (Centre) Column for the invasion of Zululand.

On its way through Pietermaritzburg Elizabeth Jones apparently became ill and died. Jones had rejoined his company by the time the Column crossed the Mzinyathi River into Zululand on 11 January 1879. B Company was left to guard the Drift and supply depot which had been established at the mission station at Rorke's Drift. Shortly after noon on the

22nd the camp of the Centre Column at Isandlwana was attacked and overrun by the Zulus; at about 4.30 p.m. the post at Rorke's Drift came under attack from elements of the Zulu reserve, who had crossed the Mzinyathi River. Jones and five other able-bodied men were posted in the hospital building to defend the patients. He took an active part in the battle, evacuating the patients room by room under intense pressure from the Zulus. Jones was recommended for the Victoria Cross by Lieutenant Bromhead, and the award was gazetted on 2 May 1879.

B Company remained in the cramped and insanitary conditions at Rorke's Drift in the aftermath of the battle and Jones became ill with rheumatism. He was sent home to England, treated at Netley hospital and discharged from the Army as unfit for further service on 2 February 1880. He settled in Manchester where he married Elizabeth Frodsham, a widow with five children. The couple later had two children of their own.

Jones appeared in a number of travelling shows locally where he recounted the story of his part in the defence of Rorke's Drift. Nevertheless he fell upon hard times and in 1893 he was forced to pawn his VC. In later life he was plagued with ill-health and suffered recurring nightmares which caused him to rush out of the house, on one occasion carrying his young granddaughter in his arms. In 1912 he was found wandering the streets and was taken to the local workhouse from where his wife collected him. He died on 15 April 1913 aged seventy-three. He was buried with military honours in a common public grave in Philips Park Cemetery, Bradford Ward, Manchester.

Lane, Thomas VC

Thomas Lane was born in May 1836 in Cork, Ireland. He enlisted in the 67th Regiment and took part in the Crimean War and the China expedition of 1860. During the storming of the North Dagu Fort on 21 August, Lane and Lieutenant Nathanial Burslem of the 67th succeeded in swimming the flooded ditches surrounding the fort and forced their way through an opening in the walls. They were among the first British troops to breach the Chinese position, and both were severely wounded. Lane was awarded the Victoria Cross for his gallantry on 28 February 1863.

Lane later left the 67th and emigrated to South Africa. It is widely rumoured that he served as an NCO in the 3rd Regiment, NNC, during the early stages of the invasion of Zululand, although this cannot be confirmed. Some accounts suggest he was a survivor of Isandlwana; if he was present at all he may equally have been with the main body of the 3rd at Mangeni. He later served as a sergeant in the Natal Horse (which was recruited from – among others – the NCOs of the disbanded 3rd NNC). His VC was later officially withdrawn; although rumours persist that Lane's crime was bigamy, he was actually court-martialled in 1881 for desertion and for absconding with his horse and weapons. No evidence survives that he returned his VC, although it is now in the collection of the Royal Hampshire Regiment Museum. Lane later applied for a replacement VC – on what grounds is unclear – and was granted it. Although no official record exists of a replacement being issued, an officer purchased a VC engraved with Lane's name in a pawnshop in South Africa in 1909 (it has since been authenticated). Lane died on 13 April 1889 in Kimberley. His VC forfeiture was one of only eight ever recorded; since 1920 forfeiture has been discontinued.

Leet, William Knox VC

William Knox Leet was born in County Dublin, Ireland, on 3 November 1833, the youngest of five sons of the Reverend E.S. Leet. All five of the Leet brothers followed a military career; William joined the 13th Light Infantry as an ensign on 4 July 1855. He was promoted lieutenant in February 1856 and took part with his battalion in the Indian Mutiny 1858-1859. He was orderly officer to Major Cox and as such delivered orders under fire in a number of successive engagements.

When the battalion returned to England at the end of the

campaign Leet was appointed adjutant, a post he retained until 1864. He was promoted captain in November 1864. He was detached from his battalion to serve as Musketry Instructor at Hythe and Deputy Assistant Adjutant and Quartermaster in Cork. The 13th was sent to the Cape in April 1877 and Leet joined them there five months later. He was promoted brevet major in October 1877 and major in May 1878. Leet was present throughout the 13th's operations against King Sekhukhune in 1878 and when this campaign was abandoned the 13th was attached to Colonel Wood's No. 4 (Left Flank) Column. In February 1879 Leet was appointed to the command of the 1st Battalion, Wood's Irregulars, an auxiliary unit raised from African tenant farmers (mostly Swazis) living in the Transvaal border region. At the end of February Leet injured his knee in a tug-of-war in camp but despite this he commanded the 1st Battalion in the assault on Hlobane mountain on 28 March. Leet's men were attached to Colonel Buller's assault party which successfully ascended the eastern end of the mountain. Once on the summit the auxiliaries dispersed to round up Zulu cattle while Leet and an Artillery officer, Major Tremlett, went ahead to effect a juncture with Colonel Russell's assault party approaching from the far (western) end. They did so but found that Russell could not reach the summit of Hlobane due to the steep ascent. Leet returned to report to Buller, but already by that time the British position on the summit was deteriorating. Zulus from the local abaQulusi people had assembled on the summit and were driving Buller's men across the plateau.

Shortly after, a large Zulu army – dispatched from oNdini to attack Wood's base at Khambula – came into view below the mountain. In the scramble to get off the mountain, Buller's men suffered heavily at the so-called Devil's Pass. Leet himself managed to descend the pass but then attempted to take a direct route off the northern edge of the connected Ntendeka plateau below. He was accompanied by Lieutenant Duncombe of Wood's Irregulars and Lieutenant Alfred Smith of the Frontier Light Horse. Leet's horse was shot under him; he managed to grab a pack-horse passing by, but this too was killed shortly after. He finally managed to mount a third horse which had no bridle; Smith and Duncombe were by then on foot. They had not gone far down the steep slope, however, when they saw that the ground ahead of them dropped away in a sheer cliff; turning back they saw the Zulus in pursuit only a few yards away. Duncombe stopped to hold back the Zulus with his revolver; he was overpowered and killed but for a few minutes the Zulus were distracted, allowing Leet and Smith to escape. Smith took hold of Leet's saddle but was so exhausted that he could not keep up. Leet insisted that he climb up behind him and, despite being chased by the Zulus, succeeded in finding a route down Ntendeka and joining with the main party under Buller.

That night, back at Khambula, most of Wood's Irregulars deserted. The following morning, the main Zulu army attacked the camp. Despite his narrow escape at Hlobane, Leet took part in the battle and commanded the central redoubt upon which Wood's defences rested. He remained with the 13th Light Infantry throughout the second invasion and was present at the Battle of Ulundi on 4 July. On his return to England, Leet was presented with the Victoria Cross for his actions at Hlobane by Queen Victoria at Windsor Castle. Leet continued to serve with his battalion and was promoted brevet lieutenant colonel in November 1879 and lieutenant colonel on 1 July 1881. In May 1883 he took command of the battalion and in November was promoted full colonel. He then exchanged into the 2nd Battalion (the 13th had been re-designated the Somerset Light Infantry) and commanded it during the Burma campaign of 1885-1887.

He retired from the Army on 1 May 1887 and was appointed a CB and honorary major general. He died on 29 June 1898 at Great Chart, near Ashford, Kent.

Lysons, Henry VC

Henry Lysons was born in Morden, Surrey, on 13 July 1858, the second son of Lieutenant Colonel (later General) Sir

Daniel Lysons, a veteran of the Crimean War, and his first wife Harriet. Henry Lysons served with the 1st Staffordshire Militia before joining the 90th Light Infantry as a second lieutenant on 11 May 1878. Lysons was appointed ADC to Sir Henry Evelyn Wood and served with him in the closing stages of the 9th Cape Frontier War and throughout the Anglo-Zulu War. He was present when the No. 4 Column crossed into Zululand (ahead of the expiry of Sir Bartle Frere's ultimatum) on 6 January 1879.

On 28 March, elements of Wood's command assaulted the Zulu stronghold at Hlobane mountain; Wood himself followed in the wake of the assault party commanded by Lieutenant Colonel Buller. Buller's party came under fire as it ascended the mountain but successfully fought its way through to the summit. Following shortly after, Wood came across part of Buller's command – Weatherley's Border Horse, who had become separated in the confusion of the attack – closely engaged with Zulu snipers concealed among the boulders at the foot of the cliffs which surrounded the summit. Wood was accompanied by just his personal staff, including Lysons, an escort of eight men of the Mounted Infantry, and the Zulu Prince Mthonga kaMpande and his retainers. According to Wood, his interpreter, Llewellyn Lloyd, was hit and mortally wounded; Wood ordered Weatherley's men to advance to clear out the Zulu marksmen but they refused. A survivor of the Border Horse, however, reported that there was no reluctance on their part and Wood recklessly exposed his staff to an unnecessary risk. Whatever the truth, Wood's staff officer, Captain Campbell, ran towards a crevice in the rocks, where Zulus were concealed, followed by Lysons and the escort. As he entered the cave Campbell was shot through the head and killed. Lysons and one of the escort, Private Edmund Fowler, stepped over the body and fired into the cave, driving the defenders out through holes between the boulders further back. Lysons guarded the entrance of the cave for a few minutes while Fowler and other members of the escort carried Campbell's body down the slope. Wood insisted that both

Campbell and Lloyd be buried despite skirmishing still going on around them. Wood then withdrew from the field and, while riding back to the camp at Khambula, his attention was drawn by Prince Mthonga to a large Zulu army approaching from the direction of oNdini. Wood sent Lysons ahead to warn Colonel Russell's detachment, situated at the western end of Hlobane; Lysons himself did not return to Khambula until 7 p.m. that evening.

The following day the Zulu army attacked Khambula and Wood spent much of the battle directing the defences from an exposed position outside the entrenchments. His staff, including Lysons, attended him. At one point a company of the 13th Regiment was withdrawn from a position in the cattle-laager which had suffered heavily from Zulu cross-fire; during the retreat a man fell wounded. Wood started forward himself to help him, but Captain Maude of the 90th observed 'Really it isn't your place to pick up single men', and he and Lysons ran forward under fire to bring the man in. Lysons continued to serve with Wood throughout the war and was present at the final Battle of Ulundi.

In 1882 both Lysons and Fowler were awarded the Victoria Cross for the incident among the boulders at Hlobane.

Lysons was promoted lieutenant in December 1879 and served as adjutant of the 90th between 1880 and 1882. He served in India and in the Egyptian campaign of 1882 and was employed with the Anglo-Egyptian Army during the Gordon Relief Expedition (1885). He then enjoyed a number of staff posts in England and Ireland, was promoted captain in 1886, passed through Staff College in 1890, and married Miss Wanda Treffry. In 1898 he transferred to the Royal Fusiliers and in December 1900 was appointed lieutenant colonel commanding the 1st Battalion Bedfordshire Regiment. His last posting was to India. He retired a full colonel in 1906. He died in London on 24 July 1907, shortly after his forty-ninth birthday.

MacLeod, Norman Magnus

Norman MacLeod was the eldest son of Norman MacLeod of Dunvegan, Isle of Skye, and his wife Louisa. He was born in London on 29 July 1839 and educated at Harrow before entering the 74th Regiment as an ensign in March 1858. He served with the regiment in India, Gibraltar and Malta, and resigned in 1872 with the rank of captain. In July 1873 he joined relatives living in Natal for a hunting expedition in Zululand, during which he attended the 'coronation' of King Cetshwayo. He enjoyed life in southern Africa, and over the next few years undertook further hunting trips and travelled to India to represent Natal's labour interests. During the political crisis that led to the invasion of Zululand, MacLeod volunteered his services to Sir Bartle Frere, and was appointed as a political agent for the Utrecht district attached to Colonel Wood's column.

MacLeod's responsibilities included raising a force of black police from among Swazi tenants living on the border farms, and opening negotiations with the Swazi king, Mbandzeni waMswati, with a view to securing Swazi support against the Zulu. MacLeod established himself at the hamlet of Derby, close to the border. Shortly afterwards Colonel Rowlands' No. 5 Column camped in the same area, causing some awkwardness with MacLeod who remained responsible to Wood's command. MacLeod spent much of the war in frustrating negotiations with the Swazi king; the Swazis made promises of support but were determined not to commit themselves to the war until the British ascendancy was secured. MacLeod also took part in some of the skirmishing conducted by Rowlands' troops. His greatest diplomatic success was the part he played in securing the surrender of Prince Hamu kaNzibe, the only member of the Zulu Royal House who defected to the British throughout the war. MacLeod escorted Hamu out of Zululand at the beginning of March.

After the Battle of Ulundi, MacLeod finally persuaded the Swazis to enter the war and Swazi troops were assembled on the Phongolo River with the intention of supporting the last pacification operations and of joining the hunt for the fugitive King Cetshwayo. In the event, both MacLeod and General Sir Garnet Wolseley were reluctant to authorize their use for fear of the humanitarian repercussions and they took part in only a limited number of skirmishes. After the capture of King Cetshwayo of 28 August the Swazis dispersed. With the end of the Anglo-Zulu War, Wolseley moved to the Transvaal with the intention of resolving the long-standing dispute with the Pedi of King Sekhukhune woaSekwati. MacLeod was again asked to call upon Swazi assistance and this time King Mbandzeni agreed. On 28 November MacLeod personally accompanied a Swazi impi which captured the Pedi capital of Tsate. After the Pedi campaign MacLeod returned to Britain and was awarded a CMG for his services. He married Emily Isham in 1881 and in 1895 became chief of the Clan MacLeod. He died in Horsham, Sussex, on 5 November 1929.

Marshall, Frederick

Sir Frederick Marshall was born on 26 July 1829 in Edenbridge, Kent, and was commissioned as a cornet in the 10th Hussars in September 1849. He transferred to the 1st Dragoons and was promoted lieutenant in September 1851. He took part in the Crimean War as ADC to Sir James Scarlett. He was promoted captain in February 1859, major in 1863, lieutenant colonel in 1864, colonel in 1868 and major general in 1877. He married Adelaide Howard in 1861. He was commanding officer of the 2nd Life Guards between 1864 and 1873. In February 1877 he was one of four major generals sent to Natal to assist Chelmsford in the aftermath of Isandlwana. He was given command of the Cavalry Brigade – consisting of the 1st Dragoon Guards and 17th Lancers – attached to the 2nd Division.

On 21 May 1879 Marshall commanded the expedition to the old Isandlwana battlefield, which partially buried some of the dead and carried away the serviceable wagons. On 2 June he accompanied the cavalry detachments, which recovered the body of the Prince Imperial of France, killed in the Itshotshozi valley the day before. The Cavalry Brigade played a prominent role during the second invasion, screening the advance of the 2nd Division and destroying Zulu homesteads. On 4 July the 17th Lancers played a decisive part in the final destruction of the Zulu army at the Battle of Ulundi. The brigade was disbanded after the battle but Chelmsford's successor, Sir Garnet Wolseley, placed Marshall in charge of advanced posts and lines of communication. After the war, Marshall was promoted lieutenant general (1884) and was appointed to the command of 1st Dragoon Guards in 1890. He was invested as a KCMG and knighted in 1897. He died on 8 June 1900 at the age of seventy.

Marter, Richard James Coombe

Richard Marter was born in 1838, the son of the Reverend R. Marter, rector of Bright Waltham, Berkshire. He entered the Army in 1851, was gazetted lieutenant in 1853, captain in 1862 and major in 1877. In 1859 he married the daughter of a colonel of the Madras Artillery. He was serving with the 1st (King's) Dragoon Guards when the regiment, stationed at Aldershot, received orders on 12 February 1879 to sail for Natal. Marter commanded the left wing of the regiment, which sailed from Southampton on the transport *Spain* on 27 February. The right wing and headquarters followed a day later, but both detachments arrived in Durban on 8 April. They then marched to Pietermaritzburg and Dundee before joining General Marshall's Cavalry Brigade, which was attached to the 2nd Division.

The Brigade took part in the burial of the dead at Isandlwana on 21 May 1879, and on the 27th two squadrons under Marter made an extended reconnaissance into Zululand. Marter, indeed, was to have an active war, for while most of the regiment was destined to be deployed on the lines of communications, Marter's squadrons accompanied the general advance. They were present during the recovery of the body of the Prince Imperial on 1 June, and during the cavalry encounter at eZungeni on 6 June, in which Lieutenant Frith, the adjutant of the 17th Lancers, was killed. Marter's Dragoons were employed to cover the retreat of the Lancers at the end of the affair. On 17 June Marter's detachment was ordered to Fort Newdigate and, as the senior officer present, Marter commanded the fort for several days. From Fort Newdigate, Marter's detachment made regular and extended patrols into Zululand, destroying Zulu homesteads, and during this time Marter and three of his men erected a monument on the spot where the Prince Imperial was killed.

After the Battle of Ulundi, and the arrival of Sir Garnet Wolseley, the British columns were reorganized and Marter's squadrons were attached to Lieutenant Colonel Clarke's column. During this time detachments of the Dragoons were repeatedly employed in an attempt to locate the fugitive King Cetshwayo. On 23 August Clarke established an advanced camp north of the Black Mfolozi to use as a base in such operations. On the night of the 26th he received information that the king was moving towards the Ngome forest. He ordered Major Marter to lead a detachment, consisting of a squadron of Dragoons, a company of NNC and detachments of the Mounted Infantry and Lonsdale's Horse to intercept him.

Marter set out early on the morning of the 27th, moving north up the course of the Vuna River. This was difficult and sparsely populated country, but the following morning the patrol encountered a Zulu who, in conversation, hinted broadly that 'I have heard the wind blows from this side today, but you should take that road until you come to Nisaka's kraal'. Marter took his advice, and en route encountered a runner with a message in a cleft stick, hurrying between other British patrols, which were also closing in. Marter pressed on to Nisaka's homestead, and then onto a steep ridge beyond. In the valley below, a small homestead known as kwaDwasa could be seen, and Marter guessed this was where the king had taken refuge. Marter ordered his men to take off their steel scabbards and any other noisy kit and, leaving a small detachment to guard them, he led the Dragoons down into the valley by a steep and winding route. The NNC were sent down a more direct path, concealed by bush. The Dragoons reached the valley at about 3 p.m., then dashed into the open to surround kwaDwasa where they were joined by the NNC. The inhabitants of the homestead were taken by surprise; they proved to be the king and his attendants. Marter escorted them from the huts and that night they camped at another deserted homestead further down the valley. The following morning they met a patrol under Lord Gifford, who had come within an ace of finding the king first. Marter escorted his charges towards oNdini, where Wolseley was camped. One night several of the king's attendants tried to escape; the Dragoons fired after them and two men were killed. Marter escorted the king into Wolseley's camp on 31 August.

The capture of King Cetshwayo earned Marter a brevet lieutenant colonelcy and considerable laurels. In 1883 he took up a post as ADC to Queen Victoria which he held until 1888, when he retired from the Army with the rank of major general. He died in May 1902.

Melvill, Teignmouth VC

Melvill was born in London on 8 September 1842, the younger son of Philip Melvill, formerly of the East India Company, and his wife Eliza. Melvill was educated at Harrow, Cheltenham and Cambridge; he graduated with a BA in 1865, the year he joined the Army. He was gazetted as a lieutenant in the 1st Battalion, 24th Regiment in December 1868. He served with the battalion in Ireland, Malta and Gibraltar and, from January 1875, at the Cape. In February 1876 he married Sarah Elizabeth Reed and the couple had two sons. He was appointed adjutant of the battalion and served in the opening stages of the 9th Cape Frontier War. In 1878 he had returned to England to take up a place at the Staff College but, hearing of a fresh outbreak on the Frontier, offered to return to Africa. He served throughout the later phase of the war, the so-called Gcaleka revolt.

At the end of 1878 the 1st Battalion was attached to the No.

3 or Centre Column which assembled at Helpmekaar on the Biggarsberg heights and crossed into Zululand at Rorke's Drift on 22 January 1879. Melvill was present with the battalion in the camp at Isandlwana when it was attacked on the 22nd. He is known to have ridden about the field delivering orders from the senior officer of the battalion, Colonel Pulleine. Contrary to popular belief, there is no evidence one way or the other as to whether Melvill was ordered by Pulleine to save the Queen's Colour of the battalion. The main battlefield purpose of colours in 1879 was to serve as a rallying point at a time of crisis and, as adjutant, care of the colours would have been Melvill's duty. He may, under orders or on his own initiative, have taken the colour with a view to rallying the battalion as the British line collapsed; given the speed with which the position deteriorated that may not have been possible, and saving the colour – with its associations of battalion honour and prestige – became the only option.

Melvill rode out of the camp with the cased colour across the saddle. Somewhere on the heights above the Mzinyathi River he met Lieutenant Coghill of the same battalion, attached to the column staff, and the two attempted to ford the flooded river at Sothondose's (later Fugitives') Drift. Coghill crossed safely but Melvill was unhorsed and, still clutching the colour, clung to a rock mid-stream where an NNC officer, Lieutenant Higginson, joined him. Coghill saw their plight and returned to the water; as he did so, his horse was hit by a Zulu bullet. Melvill, Coghill and Higginson succeeded in helping each other across the river but the colour was lost in the process. The three officers struggled up the steep slopes on the Natal bank until Higginson left them to look for horses; a few minutes later Melvill and Coghill were overtaken and killed. The bodies were discovered on 4 February by a patrol from Rorke's Drift and buried initially where they fell. The colour was found in the bed of the river, jammed among the rocks. Melvill and Coghill were later reburied a few yards away at the foot of a large boulder; Sir Bartle Frere erected a cross at the spot.

The 'dash with the colours' caught the public attention in the UK as being one of the first dramatic and heroic acts from the battle which could be identified. Since there was no provision for the posthumous award of the Victoria Cross in 1879, it was merely announced that Melvill and Coghill's gallantry would have been recognized 'had they survived'. Both Melvill's widow, Sarah, and Coghill's father petitioned repeatedly on their behalf and in 1906 the rules regarding the award of the VC were changed. Among the first batch of posthumous VCs awarded retrospectively were two sent to the families of Melvill and Coghill.

Melvill and Coghill's grave was vandalized in 1973; Frere's cross was originally removed at that time as being too damaged to repair but was recently replaced at the head of the grave.

Milne, Archibald Berkel

Milne was born on 2 June 1855, the second son of Alexander Milne CB who was twice First Sea Lord of the Admiralty. Milne was educated at Wellington College and followed his father into the Navy. In 1878, serving as a lieutenant on HMS *Active*, he was part of a Naval Brigade put ashore to assist in the invasion of Zululand. Milne was attached to Lord Chelmsford's staff as an ADC. He served with the staff throughout the war and was present with Lord Chelmsford during the sweeps through the hills above the Mangeni gorge on 22 January. At one point shortly after midday Lord Chelmsford ordered Milne to climb a hillside and look back at the camp at Isandlwana through his powerful naval telescope. Since Chelmsford was at that point between the Magogo and Silutshana hills, Milne climbed the northern flank of Magogo. Looking towards Isandlwana, his view of the iNyoni ridge – from which the Zulu attack developed – was blocked by an intervening shoulder of Silutshana, and although he could plainly see the tents, shimmering in the haze, he could see no sign of a battle, and his report reassured Lord Chelmsford that nothing unusual was happening at the camp.

Later in the war, Milne was slightly wounded by a Zulu bullet while riding beside Chelmsford inside the British square at the Battle of Ulundi. In 1882 Milne was flag lieutenant to Admiral Hoskins during the operations off the coast of Egypt. On his return to British waters Milne served upon a succession of royal yachts. He was popular in Court circles and served on the staff of no less than four kings, from Edward VII to George VI. In 1905 he was appointed second in command of the Atlantic Fleet and in 1912 commander of the Mediterranean Fleet with the rank of admiral. In 1914, on the outbreak of war in Europe, Milne was instructed to prevent two German warships, the *Goeben* and *Breslau*, from passing through the Dardanelles en route to Turkey. Owing to ambiguous orders and conflicting priorities, Milne failed to prevent their passage. The arrival of the two ships in Constantinople was a significant factor in Turkey's decision to enter the war on the German side. Milne's actions provoked a controversy, which he hotly contested throughout the remainder of his life. He was recalled and after the war placed on the retired list. In 1876 his father had been knighted and, since Milne's elder brother died as a child, the baronetcy passed to him in 1896. He died on 5 July 1938 at the age of eighty-three.

Mitford, Bertram

Bertram Mitford was born on 13 June 1855, the third son of E. L. Osbaldeston Mitford of Mitford Castle, Northumberland. He was educated at the Royal Naval School, New Cross, and Hurstpierpoint College, Sussex, and he emerged with interests typical of his time and class. He enjoyed shooting, fishing and hiking and these healthy outdoor pursuits inculcated in him an interest in travel. He visited India and East Africa in search of big game and adventure – he was elected a Fellow of the Royal Geographical Society – and in 1874 he went to southern Africa to try to make his living as a stock-farmer. In 1878, however, he abandoned this in favour of a post with the Cape Civil Service. This introduced him to the unsettled state of the frontier at that time, and to the interaction between Imperialism and indigenous African societies.

In 1882, Mitford published his first book, a collection of patriotic poems in the fashion of the times entitled *Our Arms in Zululand*. That same year he undertook a trip by wagon into Zululand which resulted in his important travelogue, *Through the Zulu Country; Its Battlefields and its People*. Such was the interest generated by the war of 1879 that Mitford was not the only, or even the first, traveller to make such a journey but what distinguishes him from his rivals is the extent of his travels – he visited all the recent battlefields, not merely those which lay on the easy trade routes – and his willingness to listen to the people he met there. His account furnishes not only vivid descriptions of the sites, with the ruin of battle still upon them, but also descriptions and interviews with Zulus who participated in the war. These included ordinary warriors as well as men of significance like Prince Dabulamanzi kaMpande, Vumandaba kaNthati and Mehlokazulu kaSihayo. Moreover, unlike most contemporary officials and travellers, Mitford did not allow his own preconceptions to colour the opinions he received, and his book remains an important primary source for the Zulu perspective on the war. After his travels, he returned to the Eastern Cape and concentrated on a literary career. Between 1886 and 1888 he was proprietor of the *East London Advertiser*, and he went on to write over forty novels. These were usually tales of adventure but, while they bear comparison with the works of G. A. Henty and H. Rider Haggard, they were written for a more adult audience than Henty's, and lack Haggard's brooding mysticism. Many of Mitford's books drew on his personal knowledge of the history of the Cape Frontier and of Zululand. Although their literary style is quaint by modern standards they reveal a greater insight into the predicament of African societies than is present in Haggard, and Mitford, although essentially a member of the colonial establishment himself, was prepared to acknowledge the limitations of Imperial ideology. He spent part of his later life in Britain, and died in 1914.

Newdigate, Edward

Sir Edward Newdigate was born at Astley Castle, Warwick, in 1825. He entered the Royal Military College at Sandhurst and joined the Rifle Brigade in 1842. He was promoted lieutenant in 1846, captain in 1852, major in 1855, lieutenant colonel in 1861, colonel in 1867 and major general in 1877. He served in the Crimean War and in Canada after which he enjoyed a series of home appointments at Aldershot, Carlisle, Winchester and Chatham. He married Anne Garnier in June 1858. In February 1879 he was one of four major generals dispatched to Natal to assist Lord Chelmsford in the aftermath of Isandlwana. He was appointed to the command of the 2nd Division which was largely made up of reinforcements recently arrived from the UK. Chelmsford's decision to accompany this force largely robbed Newdigate of a meaningful role, although he accompanied the Division throughout the war and was present at the Battle of Ulundi. He returned to England after the war and commanded the South-Eastern District until 1885. He was promoted lieutenant general in 1887 and the same year changed his name to 'Newdegate' by royal licence. He was Governor of Bermuda from 1888 to 1892. He died in 1902.

Pearson, Charles Knight

Pearson was born in Yeovil, Somerset, in July 1834, the son of Commander Charles Pearson RN. In November 1852 he purchased a commission in the 99th Regiment as an ensign, and a year later transferred to the 31st. When the 31st was dispatched to the Crimea to fight the Russians, Pearson was present as a lieutenant and adjutant. He was present throughout the siege and fall of Sevastopol, and was mentioned in dispatches for his part in the attack on the Redan on 8 September 1855. At the end of the war he went on half-pay with the rank of captain, but in 1857 transferred back to the active list with a commission in the 3rd Regiment (the Buffs). Thereafter his promotion was steady – major in 1865, lieutenant colonel in 1867, colonel in 1872. In 1866 he married

Marian Mundy.

In 1876 the Buffs was ordered to the Cape. On the way out, the transport, the *St Lawrence*, ran aground at Paternoster Point, about ninety miles north of Cape Town. The men were landed safely, but spent two very uncomfortable nights ashore until they were rescued by HMS *Active*. Pearson was commended for his calm handling of a tense and potentially disastrous situation. With the Buffs settled into the Natal garrison, Pearson was made Commandant of Natal, a post he held until September 1878. By that stage, war with the Zulus was imminent, and Lord Chelmsford was making his preparations for the invasion. Pearson was offered a staff post as commander of the No. 1 Right Flank Column, and he retired from his regimental command on half pay in order to accept. Ironically, the Buffs would, in any case, form part of his command.

Pearson's column assembled at the Lower Thukela Drift at the end of 1878, and an earthwork commanding a knoll overlooking the crossing was named Fort Pearson in his honour. Heavy rainfall throughout December meant that the river itself was the first of Pearson's obstacles, and there was some difficulty establishing a hawser on the Zulu bank upon which to anchor the pont. It was not until 12 January – a day after the ultimatum expired – that Pearson began to cross, and it took several days to ferry his transport wagons across. The road ahead of him was one of the best established traders' tracks in Zululand, and it meandered through open, undulating country, across scores of rivers and streams, towards the abandoned mission station at Eshowe, twenty-five miles away as the crow flies. Eshowe was Pearson's first objective; he was directed by Chelmsford to establish a supply depot there before coordinating any further advance with the progress of the other columns.

Pearson began his advance from the Thukela on 18 January. By the 21st he had reached the vicinity of the kwaGingindlovu royal homestead and he dispatched a patrol, which found it deserted, and put it to the torch. The advance was a slow

150

business because the wet state of the country hampered the wagons. At dawn on the morning of the 22nd, the head of his column reached the Nyezane River. Beyond the river the country rose up towards the undulating plateau where Eshowe was built. Pearson sent scouts across the river into the hills, and began the laborious process of pushing his wagons across the river. At about 8 a.m. a patrol of the NNC spotted Zulu scouts on the flank of a high hill known as Wombane, to the right of the road. When they went to investigate, they blundered into the concealed advanced guard of a Zulu army which had in fact been shadowing them since the previous day, and which now lay behind Wombane. The encounter brought forward the main Zulu body, which ran down the slopes towards the straggling British column.

An attack on a column on the march was the event every British commander dreaded, because of the difficulty of defending an extended wagon train against a highly mobile enemy. In fact, however, Pearson reacted promptly, deploying his infantry in a firing line along the road, facing towards Wombane. When the Zulu centre occupied a homestead further up the track, Pearson turned his flank to face it. Although the Zulu advance was determined, their numerical advantage was unusually slim (Pearson commanded about 2,000 men while the Zulu force numbered 6,000), and insufficient to overcome the storm of rifle, artillery, rockets and Gatling machine guns they faced. After about forty-five minutes the Zulu attack stalled and Pearson directed his left to advance and clear the Zulu homestead. This precipitated a general Zulu retreat. Pearson suffered thirteen men dead and a number wounded; the Zulu losses were estimated at about 400.

Pearson resumed his march shortly after the battle had ended – not wanting to give the impression that the attack had delayed him – and the following morning occupied Eshowe. The mission consisted of a church and a number of outbuildings, and Pearson took steps to protect them, anticipating that they would be employed as a depot during his subsequent

151

advance. On 26 January, however, piquet's posted on high ground beyond the mission heard Zulus shouting from hilltop to hilltop in the distance that they had won a great victory, and the following day a runner arrived with a dispatch from Chelmsford himself breaking the news of Isandlwana, telling Pearson that all existing orders were cancelled, and that he was free to act 'as he saw fit'.

Pearson held a council of war among his officers, and it was almost decided to abandon the advance and return to Natal when Captain Wynne RE, arriving late, persuaded them to stay, arguing that a retreat would encourage the Zulus and nullify the advantages won at Nyezane. Instead, Pearson decided to reduce the garrison, sending most of his auxiliaries and mounted men – who could not adequately be fed or housed – back to the Thukela. The remainder, some 1,700 men, dug in. Under Wynne's guidance, the defensive position at Eshowe became the most extensive earthwork built by the British in Zululand during the war. The mission buildings were surrounded by a deep trench and high parapet, protected on the inside by lines of wagons.

Pearson was destined to remain at Eshowe for three months. King Cetshwayo was apparently indignant that the British had established themselves at Eshowe as if they already owned the country, and ordered that the post be invested. The line of communication with the garrisons on the Thukela River was cut, and a cordon of warriors harassed Pearson's movements outside the fort. The defences were too conspicuously strong, however, to tempt them to an outright attack.

Boredom and disease were Pearson's main problems at Eshowe. There was no room to erect tents within the fort, so the men slept each night on the wet ground under the wagons. It rained a lot, and despite Pearson's attempts to maintain hygiene, dysentery was rife. Cut off from the outside world, neither officers nor men knew how the wider war was faring. The Zulus frequently ambushed piquets and vedettes, and after a month rations were reduced.

To keep his men's spirits up, Pearson authorized a number of raids against neighbouring Zulu settlements, and on 1 March he led a strong foray that burnt the eSiqwakheni royal homestead. His dogged defence of Eshowe earned him the popular nickname 'the Bulldog of Eshowe', but some of his younger officers expressed the view that a more dynamic man might have achieved more. The siege remained essentially a stalemate, with Pearson unwilling to break out and the Zulus unable to break in.

The communication crisis was eventually resolved after the garrison improvised signalling equipment. This at last made them aware of the efforts of Chelmsford in Natal to bring them relief. In fact, assisted by reinforcements sent from the UK, Lord Chelmsford assembled a relief column which marched from the Thukela at the end of March. On 2 April it broke through the Zulu cordon at kwaGingindlovu, and the following day Chelmsford led a flying column up the steep road to Eshowe. Pearson himself rode out to meet them, and with the shaking of hands of the two commanders, the siege was lifted. Chelmsford had already decided not to occupy Eshowe as a permanent base after all, and the following morning the garrison began to evacuate it. Lord Chelmsford, accompanied by Pearson, offered one last gesture of defiance by attacking and destroying nearby eZulwini, the personal homestead of Prince Dabulamanzi.

When Chelmsford later reorganized his troops for a fresh invasion of Zululand, command of the new coastal column – the 1st Division – was given to a newcomer, Major General Henry Crealock. Pearson was made a brigade commander under him, but in fact his health was suffering from the effects of the siege, and in June 1879 he was invalided home. On his arrival in the UK he was awarded an ornate sword by the citizens of his hometown, Yeovil, and Queen Victoria herself presented him with the KCMG and made him a Commander of the Bath.

The remainder of his career was distinguished but not particularly exciting. Between May 1880 and March 1884 he was Commander of the Royal Victoria Hospital at Netley. In 1883 he was promoted to the rank of major general, and in 1885 he was sent to command British troops in the West Indies. He returned to England in 1891, was made a lieutenant general in 1891, and retired in 1895. He died in on 2 October 1909.

Prior, Melton

Melton Prior was born in London in 1845. His father was an artist, and Prior learned the basic techniques of sketching as a boy. He was attracted to the career of a professional 'special artist' who, in the days before it was possible to reproduce photographs effectively in the press, were employed to produce sketches of newsworthy events which were then worked up and published as engravings. Even as a young man Prior managed to have several sketches, submitted on a freelance basis, accepted for publication and gained professional acceptance after sketching 'a fancy bazaar ... opened by the late Princess Mary of Teck in the sixties'.

In 1873, however, he was commissioned by William Ingram of the *Illustrated London News*, the most influential weekly illustrated paper of the day, to accompany Sir Garnet Wolseley's expedition to the rain forests of Asante in West Africa. The sketches he produced immediately established Prior as a leading exponent of the art of the military sketch and, as his obituary put it, 'from 1873 until 1904 his life was one of tireless activity. In fact, it was his boast that during this period he only passed one complete year without being in the vortex of some stirring war or adventure.' Asante was followed by the Carlist War in Spain, the campaigns in the Balkans and the Russo-Turkish War. Prior's artistic style was unashamedly vivid and dramatic without sacrificing factual accuracy or local atmosphere. Ingram soon found that Prior developed a following of his own among the *Illustrated London News*' readers, and employed him to cover the most newsworthy conflicts; Prior also wrote dispatches to accompany his sketches, which reveal him as a talented writer.

Like many Victorian war correspondents, he made little pretence of impartiality, particularly when describing British military campaigns, and both he and Ingram recognized that his own adventures detracted little from a good story. In appearance and manner Prior was not particularly prepossessing, being rather short and dumpy. His eyesight was poor – he habitually wore glasses – and he was no expert horseman. He preferred to be photographed wearing a hat because he was largely bald and he had an occasionally rough manner – even his obituary, while noting his kind heart, referred to 'a certain roughness of metaphor in his speech' – and he had a high-pitched laugh which, combined with his shining head, earned him the nickname 'the screeching billiard-ball' among his colleagues.

In 1878 Prior was sent to the Cape to cover the 9th Frontier War. He had just returned to England when the news arrived of Isandlwana, and Ingram promptly sent him out again to Natal. He arrived just as Lord Chelmsford was preparing to mount the Eshowe Relief Expedition but, unusually, Prior declined to accompany it as he had a presentiment of his death. Instead, he claimed to have secured 'the services of a private individual named Porter' to sketch the campaign on his behalf; Prior claimed that, sure enough, Porter was killed during the campaign. Curiously, however, no one by that name, civilian or otherwise, appears on the roll of casualties. Prior did, however, attach himself to the troops assembling as part of the 2nd Division on the central border. Never one to suffer unnecessarily while on campaign, he hired a wagon and loaded it with luxury foodstuffs, brandy, whisky and a soda machine. On 21 May he accompanied the expedition to bury the dead on the old battlefield of Isandlwana. He produced a number of sketches of cavalrymen examining the remains that lay strewn in the long grass; when his sketches reached London, however, they were amended before publication and the more gruesome elements discreetly omitted. On the morning of 1 June – the day the new invasion began – Prior was outside his wagon when the Prince Imperial passed by; the Prince was setting off on patrol, and the two passed pleasantries. Later that evening, Prior saw a horseman galloping towards the camp in some distress, and heard the news that the Prince had been killed. The following morning, he and the other 'specials' accompanied the Cavalry Brigade in the search for the body. Prior saw the body recovered and frantically sketched the scene of the conflict; that night, he was given special dispensation to work deep into the night by the light of a screened lantern, and by first light he was able to dispatch a rider down the line with no less than nine completed drawings. A few nights later, during a scare at Fort Newdigate, Prior was almost shot during a false alarm – 'a more disgraceful scene I never witnessed, more particularly when we realized that six rounds of canister were actually fired by the artillery, without having seen one single enemy'.

On 4 July Prior was present when Lord Chelmsford drew up his troops in a large rectangular formation on the plain before oNdini. At the height of the battle, he hurried about sketching incidents inside the square, bullets striking close to him on several occasions. He witnessed a determined charge by the Zulu left on the right rear corner, and afterwards noted that 'I personally went out and reached the nearest [Zulu body] in nine paces, so their onslaught was pretty determined'. At one point he lost his sketch book – it was apparently stolen – and, realizing his work had been wasted, fell upon the ground in despair. At that moment Major General Newdigate came past, and asked him what was the matter; one of Newdidate's staff, Captain Sir William Gordon-Cumming, offered his own sketchbook, and Prior completed his drawings of the battle with that. At the end of the battle, as the Zulus withdrew, there was a rush among the 'specials' and correspondents to be first in the royal homestead at oNdini. Prior and a few companions hurried into the king's private quarters where Prior became engrossed in sketching the huts as troops set them in flames. Suddenly, he saw a figure moving behind a palisade – 'a real live Zulu, with spears and shield' – and realized that the complex was not deserted, and that he had wandered off alone. He ran back to his horse and managed to ride safely away, only to be told later by troops watching from a distance that he had been pursued by no less than five warriors. His colleague, Archibald Forbes, offered to carry Prior's sketches with his own dispatches and rode with them from the camp on the White Mfolozi that night.

After the battle, Prior returned to England but was back in Africa in 1881 on the outbreak of the Transvaal Rebellion. He arrived at the front just in time to see demoralized British troops retreating down the slopes of Majuba hill after their defeat.

In 1882 he accompanied Wolseley's expedition to Egypt; then Greece, Turkey, India, Burma, the Ndebele rebellion in Rhodesia in 1896, the Pathan Revolt, and so finally back to Natal for the Anglo-Boer War. He was trapped inside Ladysmith during the siege and produced scores of sketches of the war in Natal. In 1903 he accompanied British troops to Somaliland, and in 1904 he was present with Japanese troops during the Russo-Japanese War. This proved to be his last active campaign. He was not yet sixty, but his years of adventure had taken his toll, and he was, in any case, becoming an anachronism. Improvements in printing and photographic techniques meant that newspapers were now more easily able to print photographs actually taken on campaign. The great days of the 'special artist' were past, and to a large extent Melton Prior had embodied them. He died in London on 2 December 1911, aged sixty-five.

Pulleine, Henry Burmester

Pulleine was the eldest son of the Reverend Robert Pulleine, rector of Kirkby Wiske, near Thirsk, Yorkshire, and his wife Susan née Burmester. He was born at Spennithorne, Yorkshire, on 12 December 1838, and was educated at Marlborough College and at the Royal Military College, Sandhurst.

On 16 November 1855, he was gazetted to an ensigncy, without purchase, in the 30th Regiment, with which he served in Ireland. In June 1858 he was appointed as a lieutenant into the 2nd Battalion 24th Regiment (then being raised), and served at Sheffield, at Aldershot, and in Mauritius, where he became a captain by purchase in 1860.

In 1866 he married Frances Bell and the couple had a son and two daughters. He served in Rangoon and Secunderbad and in 1871 he transferred into the 1st Battalion as a major by purchase. During his time in the 2nd Battalion he had been highly regarded as an efficient administrator and commissariat officer. He served for three years with the 1st Battalion in Gibraltar and in January 1875 accompanied it to the Cape. In 1877 he was promoted lieutenant colonel.

When the 9th Cape Frontier War broke out, Pulleine was instructed by General Sir Arthur Cunynghame to raise two irregular units, an infantry one known as Pulleine's Rangers and a mounted unit subsequently known as the Frontier Light Horse. Pulleine served with the 1/24th in the Transkei for nearly three months, and then, in September 1878, in view of the impending hostilities with the Zulus, returned to embark for Natal; here he was appointed to the command of the city of Durban and then commandant of Pietermaritzburg. With the invasion imminent, he asked to be allowed to rejoin his regiment and set off in high spirits, riding with his groom and a packhorse and succeeded in reaching the Centre Column on 17 January 1879, which was then camped on the Zulu riverbank at Rorke's Drift. When Chelmsford marched out of the camp at Isandlwana before dawn on 22 January he left Pulleine in charge of the camp – a choice presumably dictated by Pulleine's excellent practical and administrative record. When Brevet Colonel Durnford arrived in the camp at about 10.30 that morning he outranked Pulleine but in the absence of any orders from Lord Chelmsford to the contrary Durnford decided to retain his independence of command. He was keen to take his own troops out to sweep the iNyoni heights in response to reports that an unknown number of Zulus were concealed there; Durnford asked Pulleine to supply troops in support but Pulleine, under advice from the officers of the 1/24th, demurred on the grounds that his orders were to 'defend the camp'.

Durnford left the camp without them, although his request

presumably prompted Pulleine to place an outlying company (later reinforced) on the escarpment. When news reached Pulleine of the discovery of a Zulu army by elements from Durnford's command, he deployed his troops in a screen to the north of the camp using a line of broken dongas as a defensive feature. His dispositions followed Lord Chelmsford's standing orders but were made before the full extent of the Zulu attack became apparent. These positions – further compromised by Durnford's stand in the Nyogane donga nearly a mile from the camp – proved too extended. An attempt was made to withdraw to a more secure position near the tents but the line was broken by the determined attack of the Zulu centre. Pulleine was killed during the final stages of the battle. The exact details of his death remain obscure; he was for many years identified as an officer who, according to a Zulu account, was killed while writing a letter in his tent. In fact there is not the slightest evidence to confirm this identification, and more reliable reports place him among the determined stands of the 24th on the Nek below Isandlwana.

Reynolds, James Henry VC

James Reynolds was the second son of Laurence Patrick Reynolds and his wife Margaret who ran a successful hotel in Dublin. James Reynolds was born in Kingstown (Dun Laoghaire), County Dublin on 3 February 1844. The family were staunch Catholics and there is a possibility James was originally intended for the priesthood; in fact he entered Trinity College Dublin in February 1861 as a medical student. He graduated in 1864 and achieved his Master of Surgery in 1867. In January 1868 he travelled to London to take the examination to enter the Army Medical Department; he passed and was trained in the Army Medical School at the Royal Hospital, Netley.

In 1869 he was posted to India to be attached to the 36th Regiment which was then quartered in the foothills of the 'north west frontier'. During his time in India Reynolds was required to nurse the 36th through an outbreak of cholera. His exertions, and exposure to sickness on a daily basis, eroded his own health and in 1870 he was sent back to England.

In 1873 he was posted to the Island of St Helena, and from there to the Cape.

In 1877, on the outbreak of the 9th Cape Frontier War, he was attached to the 1st Battalion 24th Regiment and took an active part in the fighting, commanding at one point the field hospital at Komga. With the preparations for the invasion of Zululand Reynolds continued his association with the 1/24th and was attached to the No. 3 (Centre) Column. When the column entered Zululand on 11 January 1879 Reynolds was left in charge of a field hospital which had been established in the Reverend Otto Witt's house at Rorke's Drift. For the next ten days Reynolds was responsible for the treatment of over thirty patients, most of whom were suffering from accidental injuries, stomach complaints or fevers.

Shortly after noon on 22 January, the garrison at Rorke's Drift heard the sound of distant firing from the direction of the column's camp at Isandlwana. Having no urgent duties, Reynolds – together with the Reverend Witt and Chaplain George Smith – decided to climb Shiyane hill, behind the post, to see if they could see anything of the action. From the summit they watched some of the fighting behind Isandlwana and saw a line of men, whom they took to be auxiliaries, moving across country to the Mzinyathi River. Reynolds then spotted a number of men on horseback riding wildly towards the mission and hurried down to see if they needed assistance; Witt and Smith soon realized that the approaching warriors were not auxiliaries but Zulus and descended after him. Reynolds assisted in preparations for the defence and, when the battle began, improvised a makeshift dressing station on the hospital veranda to treat the wounded. He continued to tend them under difficult circumstances throughout the fight with his small terrier (a Jack Russell variously given as 'Jack' or 'Dick') at his side. At one point – when the British had abandoned part of the barricade in the face of repeated Zulu attacks – Reynolds carried armfuls of ammunition to the men defending

160

the hospital building and as he did so a Zulu ball passed through his helmet.

For his part in the battle he was awarded the Victoria Cross (gazetted 17 June 1879) and promoted surgeon major. He remained at the post in the uncomfortable aftermath of the battle and was taken ill with dysentery which became rife among the garrison. He was invalided to Helpmekaar and, a few days later, sent to Ladysmith.

He returned to England in August 1879 where he was fêted as a hero. He then took up a position in Ireland where he accompanied British patrols during the land disturbances of 1879-1881.

On 22 September 1880 he married Elizabeth McCormick. From 1882 he served in Gibraltar and was promoted lieutenant colonel in April 1887, when he was sent to Gibraltar. He was appointed brigade surgeon lieutenant colonel in December 1892.

He retired from the Army on 8 January 1896 and took up civilian employment at the Royal Army Clothing Factory in London and as Medical Officer to the Cadet Company of the King's Royal Rifle Corps. He enjoyed a long retirement, marred by the death of two of his sons, George and Percy, in the First World War. He died in London on 4 March 1932 at the age of eighty-eight.

Rowlands, Sir Hugh VC

Hugh Rowlands was born on 6 May 1828 in the village of Llanrug, Wales, the second son and third child of John Rowlands, gentleman, and his wife Elizabeth. Hugh Rowlands was educated at Beaumaris Grammar School on the island of Anglesey and in September 1849 joined the Army as an ensign in the 41st Regiment.

On the outbreak of hostilities with Russia the 41st was dispatched to the Crimea, and was engaged, (Rowlands, now a captain commanding the Grenadier Company, among them), in the assault on the Alma heights on 20 September 1854. When British troops advanced to occupy positions overlooking the port of Sevastopol, the 41st was given a position on the right of the line. This was the position attacked by Russian troops before dawn on 5 November 1854 (the Battle of Inkerman). That night Rowlands had been commanding a piquet in front of the 41st's lines and found himself in the forefront of the Russian attack. The piquets endeavoured to stand their ground and as more British troops hurried to their aid a confused fight developed in broken terrain amidst the smoke and mist. At one point Rowlands saw a Lieutenant Colonel Hely unhorsed and bayoneted by Russian troops and with a handful of men, he hurried to his assistance and drove the Russians off. Rowlands himself was wounded, and was later awarded the Victoria Cross for his gallantry. He continued to serve with his regiment and played a prominent part in the attack on the Redan, where he was again wounded. For his services in the Crimea Rowlands was also awarded the Legion d'Honneur and the Order of the Medjidie.

After the Crimean War Rowlands continued to serve with the 41st in the West Indies and India. In March 1866 he was promoted to lieutenant colonel commanding his regiment. In November of that year he married Isabella Jane Barrow, whose family he knew in Wales. When, in 1874, the 41st returned to England, Rowlands exchanged into the 34th Regiment, which was then stationed in India, in order to continue his Indian lifestyle. By 1877 his period of command was nearing its end, and he appears to have felt the lack of a more active command. In 1878, Lieutenant General Thesiger (later Lord Chelmsford), who had recently taken command of British troops in southern Africa and who remembered Rowlands from his own Crimea days, requested his services as an ADC. Rowlands sailed to the Cape in early 1878, and was offered the position of Inspector of Colonial Forces. After a tour of inspection of the Transvaal garrisons, he was made commandant of the newly annexed Transvaal.

The post proved to be the most problematic of Rowlands' career, caught as he was between conflicting directives from Chelmsford and from the Administrator, Theophilus

Shepstone. In August 1878 he was directed to attack King Sekhukhune woaSekwati of the Pedi people, whose continued resistance to European encroachment had been one of the pretexts for the British annexation. Rowlands was given two under-strength battalions of British infantry and a small force of local irregulars and auxiliaries, and faced a long march in rugged terrain in the dry Transvaal winter. The Pedi refused to commit themselves to an open battle, and both Rowlands' men and animals suffered from the lack of water. After desultory skirmishing around the outlying Pedi settlements, Rowlands ordered the column to withdraw.

The failure of the expedition was undoubtedly due to lack of resources and the difficult conditions, but it damaged Rowlands' reputation in the eyes of his superiors. He was also subject to criticism behind the scenes by a number of influential officers including Evelyn Wood and Redvers Buller. While Lord Chelmsford privately regretted 'Rowlands' inaction', Rowlands himself felt frustrated by the difficult position in which he had been placed.

In planning the invasion of Zululand, Lord Chelmsford had originally intended to employ five offensive columns, converging on oNdini. In the event, lack of transport forced him to revise this plan, and two of these columns were relegated to a supporting status. Rowlands was given command of one of these – the No. 5 Column, which was based at the hamlet of Derby on the Zulu/Transvaal/Swazi border. Again Rowlands was faced with conflicting imperatives, for he remained Commandant of the Transvaal, and after the defeat at Isandlwana in January there was growing republic unrest among the Boer population. The column nearest to Rowlands was commanded by Evelyn Wood, and Wood's success in undermining him before Lord Chelmsford, was undoubtedly responsible for the leeching of Rowlands' command. Numbers of Rowlands' men were deployed to guard the settlement of Lüneburg, half way between the columns, where they effectively came under Wood's control. Nevertheless, Rowlands himself led a number of forays against Zulu outposts at the

Eloya and Makateeskop mountains, and in the Ntombe valley, throughout February. At the end of February, Rowlands returned to Pretoria at the request of the new Administrator, Sir Owen Lanyon. He and Lanyon spent several months attempting to quieten Boer discontent, and when Rowlands returned to Zululand it was not to be as commander of an independent column, but as a brigade commander in the newly formed 1st Division. He took up the post in May – effectively sidelined by Wood's growing dominance in the northern Zululand sector. He spent the rest of the war commanding the line of communications between Forts Pearson and Chelmsford.

At the end of the war Rowlands returned to a hero's welcome in his native Wales. He briefly took up a post as Assistant Adjutant and Quartermaster General in Edinburgh, but in 1881 he returned to India as commander of the Peshawar Command with the rank of brigadier general. His later career was spent between India and Great Britain, but he saw no more active service. He retired in May 1896 with the rank of full general. In 1898 he was created a Knight Military Commander of the Order of the Bath. He spent his last years actively involved in the life of his Welsh home village, and died on 29 July 1909.

Russell, Sir Baker Creed

Baker Creed Russell was born in Maitland, New South Wales, in 1837, the son of the Hon. William Russell, formerly a major in the 73rd Regiment. He entered the Army in November 1855 and was commissioned as a cornet in the 6th Dragoons. The regiment was then based at Mirath in India, and saw heavy fighting in the early stages of the Mutiny. Russell himself took part in a number of hard-fought actions. Towards the end of the war he took part in the hunt for the rebel leader Tantia Topi, and he emerged from the war with a brevet majority. He transferred to the 7th Regiment and in 1862 to the 13th Hussars.

In 1873 he volunteered to join Sir Garnet Wolseley's

campaign against the Asante ('Ashanti') on the Gold Coast of West Africa. He commanded a unit of auxiliaries which was at the forefront of Wolseley's advance on the Asante capital of Kumase. Russell was mentioned in dispatches five times, was promoted brevet lieutenant colonel and awarded the CB. Perhaps more significantly, he became a trusted member of Wolseley's inner circle, the influential 'Asante Ring'.

From July 1878 to March 1879 he was Wolseley's Assistant Military Secretary on Cyprus, and he volunteered to accompany Wolseley as a member of his staff when the latter was sent to take command at the end of the Anglo-Zulu War.

On his arrival Wolseley felt that Lord Chelmsford had failed to pacify the country sufficiently before his withdrawal after the Battle of Ulundi, and he therefore reorganized the remaining British troops in Zululand. Colonel Evelyn Wood's old command, the Flying Column, was reduced in size and placed under Baker Russell's command. Russell assumed command at the St Paul's mission on 26 July and was ordered to march north through central Zululand. His objective was the territory of the abaQulusi section near the Hlobane mountain, since Wolseley feared that the abaQulusi might continue to resist. Russell reached Hlobane at the end of August having made extensive patrols along the line of his march, securing surrenders. He received the surrender of a number of important abaQulusi *izinduna*, and in the first week of September was involved in a series of skirmishes against the last Zulu combatants still sheltering in the Ntombe River valley outside Lüneburg – the last shots of the war. It was Russell's men who, having failed to persuade Zulus sheltering in caves to surrender, blew up their caves.

With the Zulus thoroughly subdued Wolseley turned his attention against the Pedi in the Transvaal and Russell's column was marched north into Pedi territory. On 28 November it spearheaded the successful attack on the Pedi capital, Tsate. Baker Russell was rewarded on his return to England with the KCMG, became an ADC to the Queen and took command of his regiment, the 13th Hussars.

When Wolseley took command of the 1882 Egyptian expedition, Russell accompanied him as commander of the 1st Cavalry Brigade. He led the cavalry charge at Kassassin, was present at Tel-el-Kebir and the occupation of Cairo. He then took up a series of posts at home including, between 1890 and 1895, command of the Aldershot Cavalry Division. Between 1896 and 1898 he commanded the Bengal Division in India with the rank of lieutenant general. He had returned to England when the Anglo-Boer War broke out and was heavily involved in organizing the dispatch of troops to southern Africa. He retired in 1904 and died in 1911.

Russell, Francis Broadfoot

Francis Russell was the eldest son of Lieutenant Colonel F. Russell of the Madras Infantry, and was born in India on 4 September 1842. He entered the Royal Military Academy at Woolwich in 1861, graduated in 1865 and took up a commission in the Royal Artillery. He served in Malta, Canada, India and Aden before being promoted captain in 1877. He was then attached to 11 Battery, 7th Brigade, which was based in Pietermaritzburg. In November 1878 he was promoted brevet major.

As Lord Chelmsford assembled his forces for the invasion of Zululand, Russell was attached to Colonel Pearson's staff. At short notice, he was ordered to organize a rocket battery that was added to Colonel Durnford's column. Russell's battery – three rocket troughs carried on mules – joined Durnford's command at Middle Drift at the end of December. With the forward movement of the Centre Column, Durnford was ordered to Rorke's Drift in support, and he took with him Russell's battery.

On 22 January, Durnford was again ordered forward, this time to Isandlwana. On hearing of Zulu movements close to the camp, he decided to continue his advance to ensure that the heights overlooking the camp were clear of Zulus. Durnford and his mounted command rode out along the foot of the iNyoni escarpment. Russell's battery was intended to accompany them but they were escorted by auxiliaries on foot and soon fell behind. About three miles from the camp they were alerted to the sound of firing out of sight on the high ground. Russell himself rode up the escarpment to investigate and returned ordering his men to deploy for action. The rocket apparatus was set up on a knoll somewhere at the foot of the escarpment. A rocket was fired as the first Zulus appeared over the skyline but the Zulu attack developed rapidly, the warriors emerging suddenly from a donga close by to fire a volley. Russell was killed in the first shots, the mules panicked and many of the auxiliaries fled. The Zulus seem to have been the vanguard of the iNgobamakhosi *ibutho* who then hesitated to press home their attack, preferring to wait for their supports to come up. Before they could do so Durnford and the rest of his command retreated into view and their arrival allowed the survivors of the battery to escape to Isandlwana. There is no report that Russell's body was ever subsequently located or buried.

Russell, John Cecil

John Cecil Russell was born in Edinburgh in 1839, and educated privately and at New College Oxford. In September 1860 he entered the 11th Light Dragoons as a cornet, transferring almost immediately to the 10th Hussars. He held the adjutancy for five years before becoming ADC to the officer commanding the cavalry troops in Aldershot. He was promoted lieutenant in 1864 and captain in 1870 and in 1872 transferred to the 12th Lancers. In 1869 he married Hester Thornhill and the couple subsequently had seven daughters. In 1873 he took part in the Asante expedition as an ADC to Sir Archibald Allison. He was present at the Battle of Amoaful and the capture of the Asante capital, Kumase. On his return from Africa he was appointed equerry to the Prince of Wales.

In 1878 he volunteered for special service in southern Africa with the rank of brevet lieutenant colonel. He took part in Hugh Rowlands' abortive attack on the Pedi King Sekhukhune, after which Lord Chelmsford offered him command of the mounted troops attached to No. 3 Column of the Zulu field force. This, however, promptly caused friction with the Natal Volunteer units who had agreed to participate in the invasion of Zululand on the assumption that their own senior officer, Major Dartnell, would command them. Chelmsford adopted a diplomatic solution and attached Dartnell to his staff with special responsibility for the Natal Carbineers and Mounted Police while Russell remained in field command. Russell's men were prominent in the invasion of 11 January and took part in the encircling movement during the action at Sihayo's homestead on the 12th. On 22 January Russell's men scouted extensively through the Mangeni hills, probing towards the Zulu concentrations on Siphezi hill. They returned to the devastated camp at Isandlwana that evening and the following morning advanced at the head of the column to relieve the beleaguered garrison at Rorke's Drift.

Like many officers who experienced the Isandlwana campaign, Russell seems to have lost confidence by it. In March, when Lord Chelmsford began to reorganize his forces in the aftermath of Isandlwana, Russell was transferred to Evelyn Wood's command. From the first Wood seems to have been wary of Russell and certainly Russell's caution was in contrast to Wood's own commander of mounted troops, Redvers Buller. Nevertheless, Russell was given command of one of the assault parties which was scheduled to attack the Hlobane mountain on 28 March. Russell's party was ordered to move onto the Ntendeka spur at the western end of the mountain and then climb via the rocky nek – later known as the Devil's Pass – to the summit. Russell secured Ntendeka but found the pass impractical for mounted troops. He was still in position later in the day when he received a note from Wood informing him of the approach of the main Zulu army from oNdini. Wood ordered Russell to retire to 'Zunguin Nek', but owing to confusion about its whereabouts Russell took his command several miles from Hlobane.

In the recriminations which followed the defeat, Wood blamed Russell for the error and implied that the disaster which had befallen Buller's party during the withdrawal might have been averted if Russell had been on hand to offer support. In fact the error was largely of Wood's own making but Russell was increasingly isolated from the clique which dominated the command of Wood's column. Russell was present at the Battle of Khambula – he took part in the mounted foray at the beginning of the battle – but was later transferred to the remote depot in Pietermaritzburg, the ignominious result of his clash with Wood.

In 1881 he was given command of the 12th Lancers, who were then based in India. Between 1887 and 1892 he commanded the cavalry depot in Canterbury. He remained an extra equerry to the Prince of Wales and retained that position after the prince became King Edward VII. In 1902 he was made a commander of the Royal Victorian Order. He died in 1909 at the age of seventy and is buried in Canterbury.

Smith, George

George Smith was born at Docking, Norfolk, on 8 January 1845. He was educated at St Augustine's College in Canterbury and in 1870 went to Natal as a lay missionary under the auspices of the Society for the Propagation of the Christian Gospel. He was ordained deacon in 1871 and priest in 1872 by John Colenso, Bishop of Natal. He established the mission church at Weston, in Escort, Natal, in 1872.

In 1873, on the outbreak of the 'rebellion' of *inkosi* Langalibalele kaMthimkhulu Hlubi, George Smith, who had little sympathy for the plight of indigenous Africans, volunteered to serve as a chaplain to the colonial forces. He prepared his church as a place of refugee for the settler community and went into the Kahlamba mountains to bury the dead from Durnford's skirmish at Bushman's Pass.

He returned to his parishioners after the disturbances but in early 1879 again volunteered to serve as a military chaplain to the forces invading Zululand. He had arrived at Rorke's Drift shortly before disaster befell the Centre Column at Isandlwana. When news reached Rorke's Drift by means of survivors, Smith had initially planned to flee but, finding his groom had ridden away on his horse, he opted to stay. He took part in the famous defence of the mission station against an attack by some 3,500 Zulus. A tall, stooped figure with a red beard and wearing a dark greatcoat, he distributed ammunition from a haversack over his shoulder and throughout the battle sternly reproved any use of bad language among the soldiers. 'Don't swear boys', he is said to have called out, 'and shoot them!'

After the battle he read the funeral service at the burial of the bodies of Lieutenants Melvill and Coghill, and accompanied the 2nd Division as a chaplain. On 1 January 1880 Smith was appointed Chaplain to the Forces in the Army Chaplain's Department in reward for his gallantry at Rorke's Drift. He served in Aldershot and Cork and accompanied the 1882 expedition to Egypt. He remained in the Egyptian theatre and was present in the fighting around Suakin in 1884 and at the Battle of Ginniss. Most of his later career was spent in England, although he spent a year from 1903 at Harrismith in the Orange Free State. He did not marry and died on 27 November 1918 at the age of seventy-three and is buried in Preston cemetery.

Smith-Dorrien, Horace Lockwood

Horace Smith-Dorrien's long and eventful military career might easily have been cut short on his first overseas posting had he not had the good fortune to have escaped the Battle of Isandlwana.

Smith-Dorrien was born at Haresfoot House, near Berkhampstead, Hertfordshire, on 26 May 1858, the eleventh of fifteen children of Colonel Robert Smith-Dorrien. He was educated at Harrow before entering Sandhurst. He passed out in January 1877 as a lieutenant in the 95th Regiment.

When Lord Chelmsford issued an appeal for 'special service' officers in 1878, Smith-Dorrien volunteered, sharing a cabin on the voyage out with Lieutenant Henry Harford of the 99th. Smith-Dorrien was attached as a transport officer to the

Centre Column. Despite the unglamorous nature of the work, he revelled in the independence it offered him and in his first experience of the sights and sounds of a colonial army on the march. When Lord Chelmsford moved forward from Isandlwana to Rorke's Drift on 20 January 1879, Smith-Dorrien was left there but on the night of the 21st he was ordered forward to Isandlwana. It was anticipated that the convoy of empty supply wagons would be sent down the road to Rorke's Drift the following morning, and Smith-Dorrien was needed to ensure their safe departure.

In the event, the discovery of a force of Zulus in the Mangeni hills that evening caused a change of plan; the convoy was cancelled, and Smith-Dorrien was employed as a dispatch rider instead, carrying Lord Chelmsford's orders to Brevet Colonel Durnford, who had recently arrived at Rorke's Drift. Smith-Dorrien carried the orders before dawn that morning, riding alone through miles of potentially hostile territory, and only later realizing the risk. He delivered the orders to Durnford then, afraid he might miss out on the impending action, returned to Isandlwana, riding the road for a third time. He arrived shortly before the battle began and his accounts of it provide not only a vivid impression of the horrors of the final rout, but have also fuelled the controversy surrounding the question of the 24th's ammunition supply. Most famously, Smith-Dorrien recalled how he was sent, as the men in the front-line companies needed resupplying, to secure fresh ammunition, and went at first to the supplies of he 2/4th, whose Quartermaster, Edward Bloomfield, objected saying: 'For heaven's sake, don't take that, man, for it belongs to our battalion.' And I replied, 'Hang it all, you don't want a requisition now, do you?'

From this anecdote has grown the myth of over-zealous quartermasters jealously guarding their stocks of ammunition while the firing line was overwhelmed for want of them. In fact, there is more to this story than meets the eye, and Smith-Dorrien told it not as a criticism but as one 'which speaks of the coolness and discipline of the regiment'. The incident took place not at the height of the battle but early on – it must have, because Bloomfield himself was killed shortly afterwards – and the quartermaster's real concern was that Lord Chelmsford had previously ordered that the 2nd Battalion supply be kept ready for immediate dispatch should it be needed at Mangeni. Bloomfield was worried that in releasing it to a very junior officer such as Smith-Dorrien was he would be derelict in his duty to Chelmsford's orders. In fact, when pressed by Smith-Dorrien's senior, Captain Essex, Bloomfield did release his supply, which was passed to the line. In a letter home to his parents, written shortly after the battle, Smith-Dorrien wrote 'I was out with the front companies of the 24th handing them spare ammunition'. In the event, the 24th were unable to check the sustained Zulu assault and Smith-Dorrien 'jumped on my broken-kneed pony, which had had no rest for thirty hours' and escaped across the Nek below Isandlwana, fighting his way through the Zulu cordon extended to cut the fugitives off. He wrote:

> I came to the Fugitive's Drift, the descent to which was almost a precipice. I found there a man in a red coat badly assegaid in the arm, unable to move. He was, I believe, a Mounted Infantryman of the 24th, named Macdonald, but of his name I cannot be sure. I managed to make a tourniquet with a handkerchief to stop the bleeding, and got him half-way down, when a shout from behind said, 'Get on man; the Zulus are on top of you.' I turned round and saw Major Smith, RA, who was commanding the section of the guns, as white as a sheet and bleeding profusely; and in a second we were surrounded, and assegais accounted for poor Smith, my wounded MI friend, and my horse. With the help of my revolver and a wild jump down the rocks, I found myself in the Buffalo River, which was in flood.

Smith-Dorrien managed to grab the tail of a passing horse and was pulled to the other side. Here he stopped to help an exhausted civilian on the Natal bank before setting off on foot for Helpmekaar. He arrived at the post long after dark, a formidable feat of endurance – given his earlier exertions. That night he helped command the troops who manned the camp in hourly expectation of a Zulu attack.

The strain of the events of 22 January took their toll and Smith-Dorrien became ill with fever. He was transferred to hospital in Ladysmith but discharged himself in May when he heard that the second invasion of Zululand was imminent. He returned to his work as a transport officer on the lines of communication before crossing into Zululand with the 2nd Division in June. He was present in the camp on the White Mfolozi during the Battle of Ulundi on 4 July.

Smith-Dorrien's experiences may have been among the most harrowing of his military career, but they were to prove a very small part of it. He returned to his regiment, and in 1882 took part in the suppression of the Urabist revolt in Egypt. He also served in the early battles of the Sudan campaign, and was awarded the DSO after his involvement in the Battle of Ginnis in 1885. He passed through Staff College, and then served with his regiment in India, rising steadily in promotion. He was present during the Tirah campaign on the North-West Frontier in 1897-1898 and emerged with the rank of brevet lieutenant colonel. He returned to the Sudan during Lord Kitchener's 'reconquest' of 1898, and commanded the 13th Sudanese regiment during the climactic Battle of Omdurman. He was promoted brevet colonel and returned to the command of his old regiment – by then re-titled the Sherwood Foresters – in Malta.

With the outbreak of the Anglo-Boer War at the end of 1899 he returned to southern Africa, taking part in the actions on the western front during the relief of Kimberley and the advance on the Free State capital, Bloemfontein. He was promoted first to brigadier general then major general. During the guerrilla phase of the war he proved to be one of the more successful commanders of a flying column. With the end of the Boer war he returned to India as Adjutant General and General of the 4th Division, based in Baluchistan.

In 1907 he returned to England to a command in Aldershot. In 1911 he was appointed ADC to King George V, and in August 1912 he was made a full general.

At the outbreak of the First World War Smith-Dorrien was initially given a home command but following the death of senior BEF officer he was ordered to take command of II Corps in France under Sir John French. Under fierce German pressure, the BEF was already in retreat towards Mons when Smith-Dorrien arrived. II Corps reached Le Cateau on 25 August, and Smith-Dorrien was concerned that it might become cut-off. After consulting with his officers, he decided to turn and fight to ease the pressure on the withdrawal. The resulting battle proved costly to the British but Smith-Dorrien's delaying tactics were probably responsible for II Corps' survival. Indeed, Smith-Dorrien's German opponent later agreed that the battle had prevented the Germans destroying the BEF altogether. French – who disliked Smith-Dorrien personally – felt that he had disobeyed his direct orders, and had him removed from the command of II Corps. He remained in the field but following further recriminations after the 2nd Battle of Ypres he resigned his command altogether.

He returned to England in May 1915. In December he was ordered to East Africa but resigned the command due to poor health. He never enjoyed an active command again, and ended the war as Governor of Gibraltar.

He retired in 1922 and his later career was preoccupied with soldiers' welfare. The long road from Isandlwana finally came to an end on 2 August 1930 when, at the age of seventy-two, he was killed in a car crash near Chippenham in Wiltshire.

Stewart, Sir Herbert

Herbert Stewart was born on 30 June 1843, the eldest son of the Reverend Edward Stewart, rector of Sparsholt, Hampshire. He was educated at Brighton College and Winchester College, toyed briefly with the idea of a legal career, then entered the Army in 1863 as an ensign in the 37th Regiment. He was gazetted lieutenant in 1865 and captain in 1868.

He served with his regiment in India before transferring in 1873 to the 3rd Dragoon Guards. He passed through Staff College in 1878 and, in the aftermath of Isandlwana, went to Natal as a 'special service' officer. He was attached to the Cavalry Brigade under Major General Marshall and appointed brigade major. He served in this capacity throughout the war, greatly influencing the conduct of the Cavalry Brigade.

Shortly before Lord Chelmsford launched the second invasion of Zululand in June 1879 Stewart apparently volunteered a plan to make a dash on oNdini with the cavalry in the hope of taking the Zulus by surprise; this idea was rejected, and indeed Chelmsford remained cautious in his employment of the brigade throughout the war. Stewart was present in the skirmish at eZungeni on 6 June. After the Battle of Ulundi on 4 July the Cavalry Brigade was disbanded; Marshall described Stewart as 'a Brigade Major second to none in the service'. Stewart was employed on the lines of communication throughout the closing stages of the war. To his disappointment he was ordered home when Wolseley moved from Zululand to the Transvaal with the intention of attacking the baPedi king Sekhukhune; however, with the murder of the British envoy in Afghanistan, Sir Louis Cavagnari, Wolseley's chief of staff, Sir George Colley, was ordered to India, and Wolseley offered Stewart his post. Stewart served throughout the operations against Sekhukhune and was made a brevet lieutenant colonel.

In 1881 he again returned to South Africa as a 'special service' officer, this time on Colley's staff during the Transvaal Rebellion. He was present at the Battle of Majuba on 27 February 1881, where Colley was killed; Stewart himself was captured by the Boers. He returned to the UK to take up a position as ADC to the Lord Lieutenant of Ireland but in 1882 sailed with Wolseley to take part in the Egyptian campaign. He served as deputy assistant adjutant general and quartermaster general to the cavalry troops, was present during all of the minor actions of the campaign, as well as at the Battle of Tel-el-Kebir and the capture of Cairo. He emerged from the campaign with a CB and a colonelcy and was made ADC to the Queen.

In 1884 he returned to North Africa to command the cavalry troops under General Sir Gerald Graham in the fighting against the Mahdists around the Red Sea port of Suakin. He was present at the Battles of El Teb and Tamai, and for his services was awarded the KCB.

At the end of 1884, he joined Wolseley again on the expedition dispatched to relieve General Charles Gordon in Khartoum. Wolseley advanced into the Sudan, following the Nile as far as the village of Korti. Here he decided to divide his command, since the Nile entered a wide loop before resuming the course to Khartoum. Part of his force continued to advance by the river; some 1,500 men were dispatched by a more direct route across the desert. Sir Herbert Stewart was given command of this detachment. His rapid advance was not contested by the Mahdists until it reached the wells at Abu Klea. On 17 January Stewart defeated a fierce Mahdist attack and continued his advance. His troops were still harassed by Mahdist troops in the desert around them, however, and on the morning of the 19th Stewart was hit in the groin by a sniper's bullet. He was compelled to hand over his command. In the event, the column failed to reach Khartoum before it fell to the Mahdists; Stewart was invalided home by means of the Nile. He lived long enough to hear that he had been promoted major general 'for services in the field', but died on 16 February.

In 1877 Stewart had married Georgina Tombs (née Stirling). She was on her way to Egypt to nurse her wounded husband when she heard of his death.

Symons, William Penn

Symons was born on 17 July 1843 at Saltash, Cornwall, and entered the Army as an ensign with the 2/24th Regiment in March 1863. He was promoted lieutenant in 1866 and captain in February 1878. In 1877 he married Caroline Hawkins, accompanied the battalion to the Cape and served with it throughout the closing stages of the 9th Frontier War. He was also present with the battalion when it was attached to the

Centre Column for the invasion of Zululand in January 1879. On 22 January he was with that section of the 2/24th which accompanied Lord Chelmsford on the foray into the Mangeni Hills. He remained with the battalion until the end of the war. He was promoted major in 1881, brevet lieutenant colonel in 1886, brevet colonel in 1887, lieutenant colonel in 1891 and colonel in 1892. In 1882 he took up a staff appointment in Madras, but relinquished it in 1885 to accompany Sir George White's campaign in Burma. He organized the mounted infantry during the campaign and in 1889-90 commanded the Chin-Lushai Expeditionary Force.

In 1892 Penn Symons was one of three serving officers of the then South Wales Borderers – together with Farquhar Glennie and George Paton – who compiled the *Historical Records of the 24th*, which contained an enormously influential account of the Isandlwana campaign. Penn Symons' original description of the battle, drawn largely from the accounts of survivors whom he knew, was considered too contentious and was included only in modified form; the original has only recently been published.

Symons commanded the 2nd Battalion South Wales Borderers between 1891 and 1893. He was appointed Assistant Adjutant for Musketry for India in 1893, and served in the Waziri expedition on the North-West Frontier in 1894-95. During the Pathan Revolt of 1897 he commanded the 2nd Brigade of the Tochi Field Force. In the subsequent Tirah expedition he commanded the 1st Division with the local rank of major general. He was awarded the KCB for his services.

In May 1899 he was appointed brigadier general in command of British troops in Natal. He arrived at a time of high tension between the British colonies in southern Africa and the Boer republics of the Transvaal and Orange Free State. In the event of a Boer invasion, Symons felt that it was important to halt any Boer incursion as quickly as possible. When war broke out in October 1899, a strong force was dispatched to Natal under the command of General Sir George White – under whom Symons had served in Burma – but

Symons had already determined to make a stand at Dundee, in northern Natal. On 20 October Boer commandos occupied the Talana hill overlooking Dundee, and Symons made a determined attack to drive them off. Although he was successful, the British suffered heavy casualties and Symons himself was badly wounded. Command devolved on his subordinate, Colonel Yule, who decided that the defence of Dundee was impractical. Yule promptly abandoned the town and retreated towards Ladysmith; Symons was considered too ill to move, and was left in the town under medical care. He died on 23 October and is buried in Dundee.

Wassall, Samuel VC

Wassall was born on 7 April 1856 near Dudley in Staffordshire, the son of Samuel and Emma Wassall. He enlisted in the Army on 28 November 1874 listing his previous trade as dyer. He was enrolled in the 80th regiment and, in early 1878 – when the regiment was at the Cape – he volunteered to join the Mounted Infantry. He took part in the unsuccessful Sekhukhune expedition in 1878 and his squadron was then attached to the No. 3 (Centre) Column for the invasion of Zululand in January 1879. A small detachment of mounted troops was left in the camp at Isandlwana when Lord Chelmsford marched out to attack the supposed Zulu concentrations at Mangeni before dawn on 22 January. Wassall was among them. During the rout he reached the flooded Mzinyathi River safely – the border with British Natal – but then, according to his own account:

> I drove my horse into the torrent, thankful even to be in that part and was urging him to the other side, when I heard a cry for help and I saw a man of my own Regiment, a Private named Westwood was being carried away. He was struggling, desperately and was drowning. The Zulus were sweeping down to the river bank, which I had just left and there was a terrible temptation to go ahead and just save one's self, but I turned my horse around on the Zulu bank,

got him there, dismounted, tied him up to a tree and I never tied him more swiftly. Then I struggled out to Westwood, got hold of him and struggled back to the horse with him. I scrambled up into the saddle, pulled Westwood after me and plunged into the torrent again, and as I did so the Zulus rushed up to the bank and let drive with their firearms and spears, but most mercifully I escaped them all and with a thankful heart urged my gallant horse up the steep bank on the Natal side and then got him to go as hard as he could towards Helpmakaar about fifteen miles from Isandlwana, where our main camp was.

Wassall was awarded the Victoria Cross for saving Westwood's life; he was the only survivor of Isandlwana to receive the award (Lieutenants Melvill and Coghill were later awarded the VC posthumously).

In December 1880 Wassall was transferred to the Army reserve, having completed his six years' active service. He moved in with his brother William in Barrow-in-Furness and in 1882 married Rebecca Round. The couple had a total of seven children. Samuel Wassall died in Barrow on 21 January 1927.

Wells, Janet

According to family sources, she was born in 1859 in Maida Vale, London. Janet Wells was one of six civilian nurses, provided by the Stafford House Committee, and sent to Natal late in the war to cater for the British sick and wounded.

In November 1876, aged seventeen years, she entered the fledgling profession of nursing and joined the Training School of the Evangelical Protestant Deaconess' Institution and Training Hospital as a trainee nurse. She was sent to the Balkans to assist the Russian army medical teams in the 1877-8 Balkan War and was decorated with the Imperial Red Cross of Russia.

In 1879, she volunteered for service in Zululand. She travelled from Durban to Utrecht – over 200 miles – in a post cart. In her first three months at Utrecht she treated over 3,200 patients, both British soldiers and Zulus, including men injured in the Battles of Hlobane, Khambula and Ulundi. She performed numerous operations, tended the sick and wounded, and brought an air of discipline, tempered by her charm and femininity, into a chaotic and desperate situation. Towards the end of the war she was sent to Rorke's Drift where she administered to the remaining garrison. She walked the battlefields of Rorke's Drift and Isandlwana where she collected flowers for her scrapbooks, which survive to this day. She later visited – and treated – the captive King Cetshwayo in Cape Town.

After the war she returned to her home and family in London, just in time for her twentieth birthday. In 1880 she met George King, an up-and-coming young London journalist who was soon to become the distinguished editor of the *Globe* magazine and founder of the *Tatler*. They married on 6 May 1882 and she later had two daughters, Elsie and Daisy. Queen Victoria decorated her with the Royal Red Cross, then known as 'the nursing Victoria Cross'. In 1901 she was invited to the state funeral of Queen Victoria. She died of cancer at Purley in Surrey on 6 June 1911.

Williams J. *see* Fielding.

Wolseley, Sir Garnet Joseph

Wolseley was born at Golden Bridge, County Dublin, Ireland, on 4 June 1833. He was the eldest son of Major Garnet Wolseley of the 25th Regiment. Educated in Dublin, the young Garnet obtained a commission in the 12th Regiment in 1852 and transferred to the 80th Regiment. He served in the 2nd Burma War of 1852 and was severely wounded leading a storming party against a Burmese stronghold. Promoted lieutenant and invalided home, he transferred to the 90th Regiment with whom he landed in the Crimea in December 1854. He served in the trenches around Sevastopol where he was wounded again, twice, and in September 1855 he was promoted captain after only five years' service. Attached to the quartermaster-general's staff, he was one of the last British officers to leave the Crimea in 1856.

He returned with the 90th to Aldershot which, in March 1857, was ordered to China. Wolseley was commanding a detachment on the transport *Transit* which ran aground; although the troops were landed safely; they were redirected to India where the Mutiny had just broken out. Wolseley took part in the fierce fighting during the attempts to relieve Lucknow in late 1857-early 1858. He was then attached to Sir Hope Grant's staff during the mopping-up operations, and in 1860 accompanied Grant on the Anglo-French expedition to China. He had been promoted major in March 1858 and lieutenant colonel in April 1859.

In China he was present at the attacks on the Tagu Forts and the occupation of Beijing. He published a book on the war on his return to England. In 1861 he was sent to Canada and was involved in the actions against American Fenian raiders in 1866. In 1867 he married Louisa Erskine and the couple had a daughter, Frances.

In 1870, with the rank of brevet colonel, he commanded the expedition to suppress discontent among the mixed-race Metis people in Canada's Manitoba district. It was in this campaign – his first in which he was in senior command – that his flair for organizational efficiency first attracted notice. The Metis could only be reached after a 600 mile advance across wilderness territory, much of it accomplished by means of navigable rivers, and Wolseley only succeeded because of the thorough attention he gave to his logistics. He returned from the campaign a KCMG and CB.

In 1871 he was appointed assistant adjutant general at the War Office and threw himself into the implementation of Minister of War Cardwell's reforms. From this point he became associated with a progressive movement in Army politics. In 1873 he was given command of the expedition to the Gold Coast of West Africa – modern Ghana – against the Asante people. His execution of a rapid advance through difficult rainforest terrain and the capture of the Asante capital of Kumase was regarded as a model punitive expedition of the time. During the campaign he attracted a number of ambitious staff officers about him with whom he worked closely in later life; they were generally known as the 'Ashanti' (Asante) or 'Wolseley Ring'. It made him a popular hero, too, and the press dubbed him 'Our Only General' while the phrase 'All Sir Garnet' passed into common use to indicate everything being in a good and proper state.

In 1875 Wolseley went to Natal for a brief tenure as administrator, an experience which gave him a taste of local politics and introduced him to influential figures like Bulwer, Shepstone and Colenso. In November 1876 he accepted a post on the Council of India and in 1878 became Governor of Cyprus. In June 1879, however, his service there was interrupted when he was appointed Special Commissioner to Southern Africa with full military and civil powers in reaction to the prolonged campaign in Zululand, and in particular to the breakdown in the relationship between Lord Chelmsford and the colonial authorities. Wolseley effectively outranked and superseded both Chelmsford and Frere.

He arrived in Durban on 28 June and immediately ordered Chelmsford to halt his advance until he could arrive at the front to take command. Chelmsford, however, had by that time advanced deep into central Zululand and exploited the communication delays to allow himself the chance to defeat the Zulus before being replaced. On 2 July Wolseley attempted to land on the Zululand coast at Port Durnford but was prevented by the heavy surf. Before he could reach the front overland Lord Chelmsford defeated the Zulus at Ulundi on 4 July. Immediately after the battle Chelmsford ordered the withdrawal of British troops and resigned his command. Wolseley accepted his resignation but considered Chelmsford's withdrawal to have been hasty. He reorganized the remaining troops, re-occupied the site of oNdini and organized sweeps through Zululand to pacify any lingering resistance.

In his private diaries Wolseley left acerbic observations on many of Chelmsford's officers and actions which reflected his frustration at being robbed of command during the climax of the campaign.

At oNdini he accepted the surrender of Zulu notables and, influenced by colonial officials, planned the post-war settlement of the country. The administration in London had changed from Conservative to Liberal and there was no longer the political will for the appropriation of new territories in southern Africa. Wolseley's political brief was to withdraw from Zululand and to establish a new administration which would prevent the Zulu Royal House from posing a threat to neighbouring British interests. Wolseley divided the country among thirteen appointed chiefs who were believed to be either pro-British or antagonistic to the Zulu Royal House. Although his settlement was later criticized for the violence it unleashed, it was on one level brutally successful; it certainly prevented a united Zululand resisting the future extension of European authority. Wolseley had already decided upon his policies when King Cetshwayo was captured on 28 August; he had the king sent into exile at the Cape. At the beginning of September he left Zululand for the Transvaal where he planned the successful subjugation of the Pedi of King Sekhukhune whose capital Wolseley took by force in September. He returned home in May 1880 and was made a GCB.

In 1882 he commanded the expedition to suppress the Urabist nationalist revolt in Egypt and won a decisive and typically well-orchestrated victory at Tel-el-Kebir. The campaign crowned his public popularity and he was created Baron Wolseley of Cairo. With the Egyptian entanglement, however, came British involvement in the Sudan and in 1885 Wolseley was given command of the expedition sent to relieve the beleaguered General Gordon at Khartoum. Wolseley planned the advance – by Nile and by a flying column across the desert – with typical thoroughness, but lack of political will hampered him and his troops, who arrived at Khartoum too late to save Gordon. He was, nonetheless, made a viscount. It was his last field command and he turned instead to a series of important posts at home (Adjutant-General of the Forces, commander in Ireland).

In 1894 he was promoted field marshal and he schemed openly to become the next Commander-in-Chief of the British Army upon the retirement of the Duke of Cambridge. He achieved his ambition in 1895 only to find that the post was robbed of many of its powers and that his tenure was limited to five years. He used his time to push through many of the reforms which he had championed all his life and saw their vindication in the successful employment of the reserve system on the outbreak of the Anglo-Boer War in 1899. In 1901 he handed over command to Lord Roberts whose clique of India-based officers had always been held to rival the 'Asante Ring'. Wolseley died on 26 March 1913 in Mentone, France; despite his personal eccentricities, his snobbishness, his sharp pen and his open ambition, he was one of the most remarkable and influential soldiers of his age.

Wood, Sir Henry Evelyn VC

Evelyn Wood's remarkable military career took him from being a midshipman in the Royal Navy to a field marshal in the British Army. He was born in the vicarage at Cressing, a village near Braintree, Essex, on 9 February 1838, the youngest son of John Page Wood, a clergyman, and his wife Emma. Evelyn Wood – as he was generally known – was educated at Marlborough Grammar School and College.

In May 1852 he entered the Royal Navy and served as a midshipman on HMS *Queen*. In 1854 he was part of a Royal Naval landing party put ashore to take part in the Crimean War. He was present at the Battle of Inkerman and the siege of Sevastopol, and on 18 June 1855 was severely wounded in the attack on the Redan, shot down as he carried forward a scaling ladder. A piece of grapeshot, '...weighing 5.5 oz. struck my arm just below the funny bone. This sent me screaming to the ground.' A surgeon wanted to amputate his arm but Wood dissuaded him. After treatment in the hospital at Scutari, Wood was invalided home but, being keen to see further action and doubtful that the Navy would be employed, he decided to transfer to the Army and joined the 13th Light Dragoons as a cornet in September 1855. In February he was promoted lieutenant and October 1857 transferred to the 17th Lancers in the hope of taking part in the Indian Mutiny. In 1858 he took part in Sir Hugh Rose's campaign against Tantia Topi in central India. On 19 October 1858 he distinguished himself leading a charge and almost single-handedly routed a group of rebel sepoys, an action for which he was later awarded the Victoria Cross. Being entertained one day by a Nawab, Wood was shown his private menagerie, which included a giraffe and agreed to ride it for a bet. He was just dismounting when the animal knocked him over and:

> ...his hind foot came down on my face, and knocked me insensible, cutting a hole in either cheek and in my lip, and making a mash of my nose. For the next three days I was carried in a dooly.

Towards the end of the Mutiny, Wood was attached to an Indian regiment, Beatson's Irregular Horse, and took part in policing operations. In 1860 he returned to England where he met Mary Pauline Southwell, whom he married in 1867. Meanwhile, in 1861 he joined the Staff College and became a captain and, in 1862, a brevet major, exchanging about the same time into an infantry regiment, the 73rd Highlanders (he returned to the cavalry three years later). He was given staff appointments in Ireland (ADC) and Aldershot (Deputy Assistant Adjutant General) and in 1871 transferred again to the 90th Light Infantry.

In January 1873 he was promoted brevet lieutenant colonel and later that year joined Sir Garnet Wolseley's Asante expedition as a special service officer at Wolseley's request. He raised Wood's Regiment, a unit of African auxiliaries, and took part in the advance on the Asante capital of Kumase. In the forest fight at Amoaful 'an Ashanti lying close to me shot the head of a nail into my chest immediately over the region of the heart'.

The wound was not a serious one and Wood was able to rejoin the column in time to be present at the capture of Kumase. He emerged from the campaign a brevet colonel and a CB, and a member of Wolseley's influential 'Ashanti Ring'. He returned to staff posts in England but in early 1878 the 90th was dispatched to southern Africa and Wood followed it to take up command. He sailed on the same ship as Lieutenant General Sir Frederic Thesiger – later Lord Chelmsford – who was due to assume command of British troops at the Cape. When they landed in May, the ninth Eastern Cape Frontier War was entering its final stage. The amaXhosa living under *inkosi* Sandili in the Ciskei had taken up arms and Thesiger embarked on a series of sweeps through the bush designed to disperse them. Wood was given command of a column that swept the Perie and Tutu bush and took part in the attack on the stronghold at Intaba-ka-Ndonda.

With the end of the Frontier campaign Lord Chelmsford redeployed his troops for the invasion of Zululand. Evelyn Wood was given command of the Left Flank (No. 3) Column. This column was operating in sparsely populated border districts where the local Zulu groups enjoyed considerable autonomy; although required to coordinate his advance with the other columns, Chelmsford allowed Wood considerable freedom of movement to deal with local situations as they arose. The choice of Wood for this column reflected the fact that he was the officer of his rank most experienced in colonial warfare. Wood was at that time at the height of his powers, a dynamic, aggressive and self-confidant commander more than capable of acting on his own initiative. As a man he was also a little vain, prone to bouts of hypochondria and intuitively political. He and his commander of mounted troops, Redvers Buller, formed a close mutually supportive clique and together they skilfully promoted their own successes and adroitly distanced themselves from the failings of Lord Chelmsford. They also excluded officers whom they regarded as a threat and played a significant part in the undermining of a number of military reputations during the war, including those of Sir

Hugh Rowlands, Captain Gardner and Lieutenants Chard and Carey.

Wood began the war aggressively, crossing onto Zulu soil on 6 January, before Frere's ultimatum expired. He established a base at Fort Thinta and made an extensive raid against the abaQulusi strongholds around the Hlobane and Zungwini mountains. He was skirmishing at the base of Hlobane on 24 January when the news of Isandlwana reached him. He retired to Fort Thinta, and then moved his camp to Khambula hill, a stronger position which was also strategically better placed for the defence of the Transvaal border settlements. Throughout February and March Wood and Buller skirmished with the abaQulusi and the followers of Prince Mbilini waMswati. On 28 March Wood launched an attack on Hlobane, timed to distract attention from Lord Chelmsford's advance to relieve Eshowe. The expedition was poorly planned and badly executed; there is evidence that Wood knew of the approach of a Zulu army from oNdini, but chose to ignore it. Wood himself followed in the wake of the assault parties and he and his staff came under fire. His staff officer, Captain Campbell, was shot dead, perhaps as a result of an error of judgement on Wood's part. Wood was clearly shaken by the incident and left the field, abandoning the assault parties to escape as best they could. The following day, the main Zulu army attacked Wood's base at Khambula. He had carefully prepared his position and seized the initiative early in the battle by provoking the Zulu right into an unsupported attack. He directed the defence for much of the time from an exposed position on the slope of the main redoubt, and at times armed himself with a carbine and joined the firing. After several hours the Zulu army was driven off. The victory was a decisive one that greatly undermined the capacity of the Zulu army to resist the invasion further; it also expunged any embarrassment that might have attached to Wood following the earlier disaster at Hlobane.

After Khambula, Wood was given the local rank of brigadier general. When Lord Chelmsford reorganized his command for the second invasion, Wood's column was re-designated the Flying Column. It took part in the advance to oNdini, advancing in tandem with the 2nd Division. On 4 July Wood's troops formed part of the British square that successfully defeated the Zulu army at the Battle of Ulundi.

Wood and Buller returned to England after the war with their reputations greatly enhanced, and Wood was made a CB. In 1880 he went back to Natal in command of the escort of the Empress Eugenie, mother of the late Prince Imperial, who undertook a pilgrimage to the spot where her son was killed. Wood managed the Empress's itinerary in such a way as to allow time to pay his own respects to his fallen friends at Hlobane. In 1881 he was again sent to Natal, with the local rank of major general, to take part in the Transvaal Revolt. By the time he arrived British troops in Natal had been decisively defeated at Majuba hill, and the home government lacked the political will to continue the war.

Wood was left to negotiate a peace settlement with the Transvaal leaders. Before he left the Cape, he attended a meeting of prominent Zulu *amakhosi* that was held at Nhlazatshe Mountain on 31 August. The *amakhosi* were divided between royalists, who complained of the failure of the post-war settlement of Zululand and asked that King Cetshwayo be restored, and anti-royalists who supported the settlement. Wood stood by the conditions of the settlement and offered no redress to the complaints of the royalists; the meeting was later widely seen as being a decisive moment in the genesis of the Zulu Civil War.

In 1882 Wood served under Wolseley during the invasion of Egypt, and he went on to create the Anglo-Egyptian Army with the rank of Sirdar. At the beginning of 1885, however, with Wolseley's advance to relieve Gordon in the Sudan imminent, Wood was taken ill and was invalided home. It was to be his last taste of active service and he spent the rest of his career in influential staff posts in England – as commander of the Aldershot garrison and adjutant general to the Forces. He was promoted lieutenant general in 1891 and full general in 1895.

He retired with the rank of field marshal and died in Harlow, Essex, on 2 December 1919.

Woodgate, Edward Robert Prevost

Woodgate was the second son of the Reverend Henry Arthur Woodgate, rector of Belbroughton, Worcestershire. He was born in 1845, educated at Radley and joined the 4th (King's Own) Regiment in 1865.

He served with his regiment in the Abyssinian expedition of 1868 and was present at the Battle of Aroghi and the storming of Magdala. In 1873 he volunteered as a 'special service' officer to take part in the Asante expedition in West Africa where he was present in a number of actions, including the Battle of Amoaful and the capture of Kumase.

In 1877 he passed through Staff College and in 1878 went to southern Africa as a staff officer to Evelyn Wood with the rank of captain. After the death of Captain Ronald Campbell at the Battle of Hlobane on 28 March 1879, Woodgate became Wood's principal staff officer. During the Battle of Khambula, Wood noted that Woodgate personally led two companies of the 90th Regiment, under the command of Major Hackett, into a commanding position at the head of a valley, as he 'knew exactly where I wished the companies to go'. After Wood's column was re-designated the Flying Column, Woodgate was appointed acting adjutant general, and served with it throughout the remainder of the war.

He was promoted brevet major for his services, and from 1880 to 1885 served as brigade major in the West Indies. In 1893 he was appointed to the command of the 1st Royal Lancaster Regiment, and in April 1898 he was sent to West Africa to raise a new regiment, the West African Regiment. He had no sooner done so than he was required to lead it in action against a minor revolt in Sierra Leone. Woodgate's health suffered during the operations and he returned to take up a command in England. Within a few months, however, with the rank of major general he was appointed to the command of the Lancashire Brigade which was ordered to Natal under Sir

189

Charles Warren to take part in the Anglo-Boer War.

On the night of 23 January 1900 Woodgate's brigade spearheaded Warren's assault upon the position at Spioenkop. Woodgate's men ascended the hill under cover of darkness, driving off a Boer picquet, but in the gloom and pre-dawn mist Woodgate ordered them to entrench a false crest. With dawn it became apparent that this position did not command the approaches to the summit from the Boer side; although Woodgate tried to rectify the error, his men were already coming under attack. Peering over rocks to observe the Boer approach, Woodgate was shot in the head by a bullet, which entered above his left eye. He remained conscious but was too badly injured to continue his command. He was carried back down the mountain but, despite determined efforts to save him, he died in the camp at Mooi River on 23 March 1900.

Wynne, Warren Richard Colvin

Warren Wynne was born in Ireland on 9 April 1843. He was the son of Captain John Wynne, RHA, of County Dublin, and the product of the Protestant squireachy established in Cromwell's time and which had such an influence on the Victorian Army. Wynne was educated in the Royal Naval School, New Cross, before gaining admission to the Royal Military Academy at Woolwich. Here he distinguished himself in mathematics and the classics, and graduated fourth in his class. The first ten graduates were entitled to apply for a commission in the Royal Engineers, and Wynne took his, being gazetted as a lieutenant on 25 June 1862. He was posted to Gibraltar for five years, and on his return to the UK in 1871 he was appointed to the Ordnance Survey. Shortly after he married Eleanor Turbett, with whom he had a son. Eleanor died in 1873, possibly from the effects of childbirth. In February 1875 Wynne was gazetted captain, and in 1876 he married Lucy Parish, with whom he had two further sons.

At the beginning of December 1878, Wynne was given command at short notice of the 2nd Company, Royal Engineers, which were under orders to sail for the Cape; the result of Lord Chelmsford's request for reinforcements for his planned invasion of Zululand. The Company arrived in Natal at the beginning of January, and was attached to Colonel Pearson's Right Flank Column. After a hard march to the front, made worse by the wet weather, Wynne arrived at the Lower Thukela Drift on 12 January, the same day that Pearson had begun to cross onto Zulu soil. On the 13th Wynne met Pearson on the Zulu bank and at Pearson's request began work planning a fortified depot to protect the stores that were accumulating there.

Of the RE officers who distinguished themselves in the Zulu campaign – Chard and Durnford among them – Wynne's contribution has been the most overlooked. He was responsible for two of the largest fortifications built by the British in Zululand, and which between them shaped the war in the coastal sector. Although the position of his first work was not ideal – it was later criticized by one of Chelmsford's staff as being overlooked by a low hill 300 yards away – Wynne was not responsible for the choice of ground, but merely constructed a fortification around an existing depot placed by Pearson. The result was a large angular work consisting of a surrounding trench with a rampart on the inside, and partitions to screen the interior from rifle fire. It was called Fort Tenedos, in honour of HMS *Tenedos*, which had contributed a landing party to Pearson's column. Wynne supervised the working parties which had largely finished construction by the time Pearson began his advance from the river on the 18th.

Warren Wynne left a number of accounts of his experiences; he wrote a professional journal, a diary and letters to his wife. From their pages he emerges as a conscientious, efficient and self-reliant officer who, like many British officers at the time, was both devoutly religious and devoted to his family. A surviving portrait shows him to have a rather lugubrious appearance with a long nose, rather sad eyes and a heavy moustache.

On the 22nd, Pearson's column was attacked as it crossed the Nyezane River. Wynne's engineers were actually working to clear the banks of the river and fortify the drift when the battle began. When the Zulu left horn made a determined attempt to encircle Pearson's line and strike at the Drift, Wynne ordered his men to take up their rifles. He formed them into a firing line and advanced steadily towards the Zulus, driving back their attack.

The column reached its first objective, the abandoned mission station at Eshowe, on the 23rd. Here Pearson instructed Wynne to fortify the post in expectation that it would remain a standing supply depot. In fact, within a few days, Pearson received news of Isandlwana, and Wynne's orders were changed. He was now instructed to fortify the post to house the column indefinitely. As a result, he created the most ambitious engineering project built by the British during the course of the war. The entire mission complex was surrounded by a deep ditch and high rampart. Screened entrances were built, including a drawbridge, while one difficult angle in the parapet was protected by a stockade. Raised emplacements were built so that the column's artillery could fire over the ramparts. Drains were dug to carry away surplus rainwater. As time passed and no Zulu attack developed, Wynne strengthened the post by adding wire entanglements, pits with spikes driven in, and range markers around the approaches. When Zulu patrols approached under cover of darkness to pull up the range markers, it was Wynne who developed an explosive booby trap to deter them. It was Wynne, too, who invested a great deal of effort into establishing communications with the outside garrisons. His ideas included a large paper screen for signalling – sadly destroyed by a gale – and a small hot-air balloon. He was also involved in Pearson's attempt to clear a new road, shortcutting the approach to the fort, and took an enthusiastic part in the raid on the eSiqwakheni homestead on 1 March.

Sadly, Wynne's dynamism took its toll on his health. On 11 March he complained of headaches and stomach pains – the first signs of the onset of the widespread sickness afflicting the garrison, which was largely the result of infected water. Within a few days he was largely incapacitated. Following the relief of Eshowe on 3 April, Wynne was sent with other hospital patients to the Thukela. He was gazetted major in early April, in recognition of his services at Eshowe, but his condition did not improve, and he died at Fort Pearson on 9 April 1879 – his thirty-sixth birthday.

Select Bibliography

Ballard, Charles, *John Dunn; The White Chief of Zululand*, A. D. Donker, Johannesburg, 1985

Bancroft, James W., *The Zulu War VCs*, J. W. Bancroft, Manchester, 1992

Bayham-Jones, Alan, and Stevenson, Lee, *Rorke's Drift; By Those Who Were There* , Lee Stevenson Publishing, Brighton, 2003

Bendall, Simon, 'A Minor Military Dynasty of the 18th and 19th Centuries', *Journal of the Society for Army Historical Research Vol. 83, no. 334*, Summer 2005

Bennett, Ian, *Eyewitness in Zululand*, Greenhill, London, 1989

Best, Brian, and Stossel, Katie, *Sister Janet*, Pen & Sword Books Ltd., Barnsley, 2006

Binns, C.T., *The Last Zulu King; The Life and Death of Cetshwayo*, Longmans, London, 1963

—*Dinuzulu; The Death of the House of Shaka*, Longmans, London, 1968

Bryant, A.T., *Olden Times in Zululand and Natal*, Shuter & Shooter, London, 1929

Butterfield, Paul H., (ed), *War and Peace in South Africa; The Writings of Philip Anstruther and Edward Essex*, Scripta Africana, Melville, 1987

Castle, Ian and Knight, Ian, *Fearful Hard Times; The Siege and Relief of Eshowe*, Greenhill, London, 1994

Clarke, Sonia (ed), *Invasion of Zululand*, Brenthurst Press, Johannesburg, 1979

—*Zululand at War*, Brenthurst Press, Johannesburg, 1984

Child, Daphne (ed), *The Zulu War Journal of Colonel Henry Harford, C.B.*, Shuter & Shooter, Pietermaritzburg, 1878.

Coghill, Patrick, *Whom The Gods Love; A Memoir of Lieutenant Nevill Josiah Aylmer Coghill VC*, private publication, Gloucestershire, 1966

Cooper, Barbara, 'George Hamilton Browne; An Investigation into his Career in New Zealand', *Bay of Plenty Journal of History*, Vol. 33, n. 2, November, 1985

Cope, Nicholas, *To Bind the Nation; Solomon kaDinuzulu 1913-1933*, University of Natal Press, Pietermaritzburg, 1993

Drooglever, R. W .F., *The Road To Isandhlwana; Colonel Anthony Durnford in Natal and Zululand*, Greenhill, London, 1992

Emery, Frank, *The Red Soldier; Letters from the Zulu War*, Hodder &